How The hell did i become the boss?

The Funniest and (Most Honest) Business Guide
You'll Ever Read

MAY 19, 2025
FRANK BROWN
FRB59PERSONAL@GMAIL.COM

Dedication

To my family – you are purposely not front and centre in this book as we are a private lot. I hope that when you read this, it gives you a better idea of what I was doing all those times that I was away. I want you to know that despite my being away as much as I was, you were the motivation. To my children – your Mom and I wanted you to have a great jumping-off point to start your own lives, and I hope we did ya good!

To my wife – you were an equal partner (and sometimes a lot more than equal!) in everything we achieved. I am thrilled that we achieved what we wanted to achieve in this part of our lives – I could not have done it without you – thank you for everything!!

Foreword

"I worked on a project for NASA."

"I was Class Valedictorian."

"I was Homecoming King."

"I once had lunch with the famous Author John Grisham."

"I have traveled to over 50 countries."

"I could watch a 3 Stooges episode for the hundredth time and still laugh like it is the first time I have seen it."

One of these things is not like the other! So let me give you some background. Recently, my company brought together top leaders from all over the world for a team-building meeting. This was a gathering of leaders from around the world, representing various countries in our global network to try and bring the company closer together as a working unit. As the President of our Canadian branch, I **had** the privilege of being part of this exclusive gathering. Before the meeting, each of us had to spill a lesser-known detail about ourselves to participate in a fun kind of ice-breaking session. You can see from the list **that** we had a lot of achievers in that crowd. And then, there was me. **I bet you can guess which one I am, but if not, I am the last one.** I can watch a 3 Stooges episode for the hundredth time and still laugh like it is the first time I have seen it. Whether it's the eye-poking, head-sawing, or Curly's infectious "nyuk nyuk nyuk," my love for those guys began in my childhood and stuck with me into adulthood. The only hitch? In the corporate world, companies usually look for the achievers from that list – not someone who'd rather watch Curly paint himself into a corner. Some of these people were doing a lot in the very early days of their careers and education while I was off either watching Curly, drinking too much, skipping school or generally just trying to have a good time the way a lot of us young guys did at the time. To quote Steve Miller, *'I was a joker, a smoker, and even a midnight toker'* although I must **admit**, drinking always held far more of an appeal for me than weed did.

For a solid 43 years, I maneuvered through the corporate world, starting as a sales rep and eventually making it to the top as Company President. What's amusing is, unlike my colleagues who resembled well-made beds, I always felt more like the messy one with a bedspread thrown over, desperately trying to hide the chaos underneath.

I have struggled with how to write this book – let me give you the background. As a kid, one of my favourite books of all time was a book about baseball entitled "Ball Four" by Jim Bouton. Bouton had a moderately successful career in Major League Baseball, but he really outdid himself with his success as an author. Ball Four has, in hindsight, become a ground-breaking book in sports. It was the first of its kind, and that kind was a "tell-all," "no holds barred" exposé into the life of a major league baseball player. He **spared nothing and no one** in his efforts to be honest and open about what life is like. The subjects went from absurd "boys will be boys" behaviour, to the poignant (veterans being told their career is over) to the outrageously funny (Manager Joe Schultz and his different combinations of swear words). It truly was no-holds-barred and was a pioneer for a genre which grew exponentially after him – sports autobiographies. Even today, his masterpiece stands up well against any of the followers as one of the best sports books ever written. I wanted to emulate both his authenticity and his "exposé-style" in my book so that you would see things entirely through my eyes because I think that I witnessed some very cool stuff in 43 years. I am going to try and keep that focus, but there is one big difference between Bouton and me. He took no prisoners – he used real names, talked about real people and as a result, lost some very good friends who didn't want their exploits published for all to see. I completely understand their anger with Bouton – these guys came to work every day and did their jobs, and a **colleague was using their trials and** tribulations to make a boatload of money at their expense. I just can't do that (although I will gladly take the boatload of money ☺). The people I worked with through the years are very valuable to me, and I do not want to throw them under the bus just to bring an added dose of reality to my book. Don't get me wrong – I value authenticity above almost anything, but not at the expense of personal relationships. I have thereby decided that in this book, I am going to do everything possible to protect my relationships. **Some characters** are just too important to the story not to use their names, so if I do use your name, you can breathe a sigh of relief because it means I am not going to cast you in a negative light. Otherwise, I will try to minimize the use of names through terms referring more to someone's position rather than their name. I will use real names at the end of the book, but that will only be first names, and it will be only to thank you for your contribution to my journey.

There will be elements of laughter, learning, and interesting stories throughout. Expect the structure of this read to be a little non-traditional – I am going to tell you in the first part about the companies I worked for and how my career advanced. That will be a brief overview of my entire career. Then the fun starts – I will show through short, easy-to-read chapters some of the learnings, experiences, colourful characters and yes, some of the funnier moments along the way. The structure will be a little bit like me – that means kind of all over the place. We will go from serious chapters talking about valuable life lessons, and that could easily be followed up by a chapter highlighting bathroom humour. I wish I was more structured, but I learned years ago not to fight it and just go with it. In addition to feeling like I was a "fish out of water," as I described above, I also had other parts of my makeup that just made me different. Those differences were, unfortunately, not beneficial to my quest for success in the corporate world – in fact, they were detriments that I came by naturally. My Dad was a very smart man. You will hear more about him later, but we always thought of him as the Absent-Minded professor. One of his best stunts was on a trip to Vermont where he got mad at a self-serve gas station that wanted him to "pay first", and he decided to leave the station in a huff without filling up. The only problem with that approach was that he forgot to take the nozzle out of his tank, and it ripped off the pump, spraying gas everywhere. They had to shut the station down to clean it all up. Oops!!! Another of our favourite Dad stories was one time when he and my mom had a party. My Mom forgot to get something for the party and sent him out to get it. He was mad (he did have a bit of a temper), and he rushed out, opened the garage and zoomed his car out to get whatever was needed. The problem was that he opened one garage door and backed out through the other (closed door). I was 1000% equipped to do the same things. I was the Absent-minded professor without the Professorial brains. I remember once, after a round of golf with friends, we had to send a convoy of golf carts back to the 17th hole to find a wedge I had left on the ground. After 10 minutes of searching, we found the club....in my bag. I had put it back in my bag and put the wrong head cover on it, which convinced me it was gone. That (and several other similar events) prompted one of my friends to quip that I needed an Assistant for my life to follow me around and help me avoid my own stupidity. He was right!!

A word to the wise – I was brought up in a time where nothing was off limits for humour, and there was no such thing as political correctness or some of the "over the top" sensitivities we have nowadays. I am going to almost always come down on the side of authenticity rather than trying to keep in mind what other people might think or feel. If the odd bit of colourful language or bathroom humour offends you, this might not be the book for you.

I expect when this is all completed, it will be a story of 1-part learning, 1-part interesting stories, several parts of humour, and unlimited passion for what I did and the people I worked with.

Throughout those four decades, I picked up a bunch of lessons – not the textbook stuff they teach you in business school but real-life, people-centric lessons. Have you ever been with someone who, during some unexpected events, exclaimed, "Somebody should write a book about this"? Well, that someone is me.

My hope is for those who are early in their careers, there is learning here to help you achieve your goals and maybe even rethink your goals (as it happened to me several times!) For those who are more advanced in their careers or even those who don't have a career, get ready for some entertaining and inspiring chapters. Most of all, get ready to find out how for 43 years nobody threw the bedspread off that unmade bed to unmask the chaos beneath.

Introduction

I was born on November 25, 1959, in Orange, New Jersey, USA. I was 7 lbs and 11 oz and, by all accounts, was one of the happiest and most outgoing kids you will meet. I was constantly getting written up in elementary school for talking too much. In 1967, my Dad, who held a doctorate in Chemistry (which always blew my mind – who is smart enough to be a Dr. in Chemistry??) decided for career reasons to move the family (myself, my two brothers and my Mom) to Dayton, Ohio. I am the middle child of three brothers. We stayed in Dayton for 5 years until 1972, when my Dad was fired from his position as Vice President of Research and Development at Dayco Corporation. (Plastics, rubbers etc.). He was 52, he was fed up with the corporate life and the politics that went along with it. He was searching for something to

14

do when he came up with an opportunity to buy a franchise in an up-and-coming employment agency called Management Recruiters International. The franchises available were in St. Louis, Houston, or Toronto, Canada. He chose Toronto because, in 1972, it was deemed one of the fastest-growing cities in North America. Thus began my family's Canadian adventure, which some of us are still living to this day. I am a bit older now, and while I didn't realise it at the time, it was remarkable what my dad did back then. He was a chemist and, at 52, had 3 young children, a single-income family, and no job. He decided to not only take on a new job, which he had never done before (employment recruiter), but he also moved his family to an entirely new country! I wish I had told him before he passed in 2002 how incredibly impressed I am, not only that he did that, but he made it work until he retired in 1992. I have been in the Toronto area since 1972, officially becoming a Canadian citizen in 2013.

You know, they often say high school holds clues about who we'll become. I fit that mold perfectly. High school was a breeze for me, fueled by boundless energy (and probably a dash of ADHD), always on the lookout for the next "adventure." I was the one always seeking the easy way out and the maximum number of laughs, and that tendency stuck with me throughout my entire career – a lack of patience for details and hard work that some of my more 'put-together' colleagues seemed to effortlessly manage. I was more interested in finding where we were going to have our next drinking binge than I was in worrying about exams or homework. Imagine if I'd ended up in a job tethered to an office from 8 to 6, like my father did. It gives me chills to think about how different my life might have turned out – I likely would have thrown it all away for something even dumber!

Now, I have been married to the same lady since 1977. Despite the numerous times we wanted to wring each other's necks, we're still going strong. When we are not driving each other crazy, we are truly best friends. We laugh at similar things and enjoy many of the same activities – friends, family, and we are both lifelong music addicts. I am stuck in the 70s and 80s for music, my wife is a bit more open-minded. Her family joined the wave of English Quebecers migrating to Toronto in 1977, and her father held a high-level position at Robin Hood

Multifoods, the flour giant of
American multinational fame.

In 1983, we tied the knot, setting
off on our journey together. We
crafted a plan based on the family
blueprints we observed – the
traditional model: Dad works,
Mom tends to home and children.
Considering our generation
pioneered the two-income family,
we count ourselves fortunate to
have navigated it mostly on a
single income. Our two kids came
along in 1989(girl) and 1991(boy)
and share a tight bond with us.
The journey wasn't a straight line;
we faced twists and turns, but in
the end, "all's well that ends well."

Now, let's zoom in on the business
side of this life journey. I am going
to start by telling you about the
companies I worked for.

Table of Contents

10 - "Oh, if only we could see ourselves as others see us."

11 - "Pull my finger"

12 – "Quality above everything else...except our jobs!!!"

13 – "Are we making enough money?"

14 - Watch people, and they will show you who they are

15 - ASIA – (The whole fkn room shook)

16 - "I don't want you spending our money like a drunken sailor."

17 - "Nobody bats a thousand."

18 - My big secret...many years ago, I won the lottery

Company #1 Kellogg-Salada Canada Inc.

When I embarked on my career journey, the path seemed straightforward – follow in the footsteps of my Father and my Father-in-Law, aiming to conclude my professional life as a high-level executive in a decent-sized company. This would allow us a very similar lifestyle to our parents and we both wanted that. The compass guiding my early career decisions was relatively simple: anything that moved me up the corporate ladder or offered a fatter paycheck would pique my interest.

I was also armed with some great advice from my Father-in-Law – start your career with a good, well-known, company and stay for five years. The reason for this was twofold. He said that as my career progressed, keeping a job with a big company for 5 years would say to future employers that I can hold a job, and I am willing to stay with a company for more than just a fleeting moment. Secondly, he said big companies give you the best training and the earlier in your career you get that training, the more use you get out of it.

This was fantastic advice. I did have to learn on my own as time went on, career decisions are not simple and many more factors come into play which you will see later in discussions about career moves and why I made them. Circumstances are always changing thereby complicating my initial assumptions that moving up and making more money were at the top of the list for important considerations.

The challenge lies in the fact that the impact of each decision affects your career path either negatively or positively, and while you strive to make the right choices, certainty is a luxury that doesn't exist when it comes to predicting the future of your career. The "right choice" is always changing. Early in my career, learning and stability were very important **whereas** later in my career, lifestyle and happiness became more important.

My initial career aspirations were built on a false assumption. Those false assumptions were gathered during my university days while I worked at a newsstand in Toronto's extensive subway system - a job that adequately compensated a college student. There was a guy from Canada Dry, etched into my memory even after four decades. Once a week, he'd stroll into our store, crack a few jokes and "shoot the shit" for half an hour, check the pop inventory, and place an order based on simple math. He didn't wear a suit; a nice shirt and pants sufficed. No heavy briefcase for him, just a clipboard. After compiling our order, he hopped back into his company car, carefree and content. That was it – the perfect job for someone not inclined towards hard work – I found my career calling!! I envisioned myself in a sales role, breezing in and out of places, armed with my company car. Little did I know that this assumption marked the first misstep in a career fraught with its share of misjudgments.

As fate would have it, my inaugural sales position was with Kellogg's, and it was a far cry from the sanitized stores and laid-back atmosphere exuded by my newfound idol - the Canada Dry guy. I still remember getting that initial job offer – a downtown Toronto sales territory and I would be paid $16,500 plus get a company car – an Oldsmobile Cutlass. Remember, this was in the early 80's. I remember feeling like I should pinch myself because this was everything I could have imagined!

There was, however, some real **eye-opening** to come my way. I found myself selling to serious businesspeople operating restaurants, hospital food service kitchens, or managing distribution from mammoth, often unkempt warehouses. These people worked on Margins and making money was a serious business. My Manager, trained by Procter and Gamble, hailed from an era where planning and preparation reached unprecedented heights. It felt like he expected me to be so put together I could predict the exact minute in the afternoon when I was going to need a bathroom break and therefore that needed to go into my "Time-text" time management system (this was a rather extensive binder allowing for all kinds of notes and one page per each day with the date pre- printed on it). This Manager, with his penchant for discipline and structure, was the antithesis of my "unmade bed" persona.

The demands of this role were beyond my initial expectations:

☐One of the first times my Manager came with me for a ride-along we had to start the day by paying an unscheduled visit to a customer easily an hour out of our way. Why? I had left my briefcase at a customer's business the previous day. My lifelong penchant for leaving and losing things reared its ugly head early in my career.

Criticism for salt stains on my shoes and the bottom of my pants seemed trivial but, in hindsight, spoke volumes about professionalism.

My Manager's boss scheduled his first ride-along with me. The only feedback I received afterwards from my Manager was that our VP of Sales was scared to death during a rather sharp turn I made because an ice scraper flew off the ledge of the back window and from the way it was described after the fact, you would think he was nearly decapitated. (He was in the front seat and the scraper was in the back) Even as I was receiving that feedback in a serious tone from my Manager, I could feel the corner of my mouth turning up reflecting the amusement I felt at the time. By the way, there was zero feedback about

how I did with my customers –
that was one of the early
indicators to me that
corporate culture really can
be ridiculous at times!

I also thought it was insane that
when two people are in a car
together and one of them feels
threatened by an ice scraper he
would not just say something. The
idea that it had to go from him to
my Manager to me was maybe an
early indication of some of the
corporate rituals that I was going
to call "bullshit" on my entire
career. The reality of working
alongside people like this bore no
resemblance to the carefree
Canada Dry salesman I had
admired. Sales with Kellogg's
required meticulous planning,
objective-setting based on current
purchases, annual target
establishment, and the art of
ingratiating myself to clients
amidst fierce competition from

other suppliers. The breezy fantasy of counting cereal and placing orders was replaced by the necessity of strategic planning and relationship-building.

The early days of my sales career were a stark departure from the laissez-faire image I had envisioned, setting the stage for a journey marked by unexpected twists and lessons learned through trial and error. I also received my first exposure to corporate culture in large organizations and started to see some of the aspects that I would not enjoy in the ensuing years.

Company #2 - William Neilson Ltd.

I previously mentioned my commitment to Kellogg's for at least five years at the start of my career. And right on schedule, at the five-year and three-month mark, I made a pivotal move, transitioning to the William Neilson Company in Toronto as a Key Account Manager for their Confectionary Division. William Neilson manufactured candy bars (our Division - we had another division that was Dairy) and some very well-known and popular ones such as Crispy Crunch, Sweet Marie, and Malted Milk.

Several factors influenced this decision:

1. **Career Advancement:** Feeling the pressure to demonstrate progress to future employers and avoid

being pigeonholed as a "career sales guy," I sought to move up from my sales rep position. A move to Key Account Manager from Sales Representative accomplished this.

2. **Shift to Retail:** Wanting to step out of Food Service and explore the broader landscape of retail, where abundant job opportunities awaited, was a key motivation.

3. **Financial Incentive:** As it often happens, money played a role. The jump from a $26,000/year salary to $32,500 at Neilson was a welcome change.

Considering my early career criteria of progression and increased income, this move aligned almost perfectly. However, what made it stand out was the strategic shift from Food Service to retail, a move more crucial than both the promotion and the financial boost combined. It was critical because moving into the Retail environment took me into the "Big Leagues" of Food Manufacturing – I was now selling to Canada's most demanding and sophisticated retailers such as Loblaws and A & P – the Great Atlantic and Pacific Tea Company. While the demands for professionalism were the highest I could imagine, the opportunities for growth once one proved he could handle the heat were immense.

One of the pivotal moments from this transition occurred in my second week at William Neilson when it was announced that the company was acquiring Cadbury's confectionary division in Canada and would henceforth be known as Neilson/Cadbury Canada Inc. While such acquisitions often lead to staff restructuring, my Manager provided a master class in leadership. He assured me only two weeks after the announcement, "You will have a job – you are not going anywhere." This demonstration of understanding, openness, and respect left a lasting impact on me throughout my career. He understood how stressful it was for a young guy who had just moved to the company. Even back then I knew in situations like that it was often "last in first out" and you could not get any more "last in" than having joined the company a week ago. I had just left Kellogg's and without his assurance, I would have been waiting for the hammer to fall putting me on the unemployment line. His words put me at ease and reinforced in me the significance of leadership communication and its lasting influence on employees. I am pretty sure he wouldn't mind getting some credit for this great

leadership lesson – Glenn
Jones....Take a bow!

It was during my tenure at
Neilson/Cadbury that I had two
very telling experiences. The first
one involved me receiving my first
big step in my career – I was made
Manager of the Major Account
Department. I had people
reporting to me! The people
reporting to me were Key Account
Managers so not only did I have
people reporting to me but I also
had Managers reporting to me –
this was high-level stuff!! This was
also where I learned one of my
first very important lessons on
leadership. I had seen Managers
all my career and even while
working on jobs while attending
university. I had told myself that if
I ever became a Manager, I was
going to be different. I had seen
some bad Managers in my time – I

actually got scolded by one "uptight suit" because we went to see a customer and the customer had such a good time, he thought she "laughed too much" during our sales call. We got plenty of support from that particular customer but the key feedback was the negative comment on the laughter – back then and even today I say "Give me a break". The Manager was a young guy who wore what looked like $1,000 suits (a lot back then) and took himself way too seriously.

I WAS going to be the very first Nearly Perfect Manager!! I WAS going to have a high-performing team that produced great results, but the big difference was – they were going to love working for me, and we were going to be good friends. I believed in my heart of hearts that this was possible.

I had 3 Account Managers reporting to me two guys and a

lady. The lady was a very nice person who was roughly my age and had a stunning appearance. Thin, blond and over 6 feet tall, she got noticed wherever she went. She was married to an Executive in a retail organization who was well-known in the industry so she certainly didn't need the job at Neilson/Cadbury. She just enjoyed doing it.

One of the guys was a good family guy who was very easy-going. In fact, it turned out he was too easy-going (in my mind) for a sales position that demanded some aggression. The other guy was also very easy-going and they were both good friends of each others'. We started out in the honeymoon period getting along just fine. All was great and I couldn't have been happier – they liked me and seemed to respond to my management style. At the six month mark, my Manager called me in. He was not only "not pleased" with what was going on under my watch, but it had become an urgent matter in his mind. I had to fix this mess I was in.

Here was the issue – the inmates were pretty much running the asylum. In my need to be liked, I was not providing any rules or structure whatsoever. What I didn't realise was that not only was I responsible for having a group that would follow and support me, I also needed to have a group that produced results. In my thirst to be liked, I was not holding them accountable nor was I helping them learn at all.

After some soul-searching, I realized that it was time for me to change things. This group needed to know that our overall success was the only way that we were going to be able to keep going.

That success required effort on their part, and support on my part. Part of that support was that I was going to be completely honest with them about where and how they fell short. I had private one on ones with each of them and told them exactly what they needed to do to keep their career trajectory in the right direction.

After a few months, it was clear that one, the lady, had responded very well and the two others did not. I had come face to face with the first very difficult decision in my career. After exhausting all alternatives, I was faced with having to terminate my first employee. In a big company like I was in, they prepare you very diligently right down to what you say, how you say it, and what you do afterwards (leave and let HR take care of the rest). I have to say, I could not sleep for a week before that. I knew this guy, I knew his family, and I knew they had a young toddler. He was a very nice guy – he just didn't put out the kind of effort that was required for that position despite having been told many times what was needed. On the day of the termination, I was literally shaking when it came time. I read my script, said Goodbye and that was that.

Human Resources then took him through his severance letter and set him up with some career counselling. I then had to deal with the after-effects which were minimal when compared to the lead up to that day. To this day, that was probably the toughest thing I have ever had to do in business. I won't say it gets easier, but I will say you gain an understanding in time. The understanding is that well before it reaches that point, the employee has many chances to avoid that situation. They can take the corrective action recommended or they can fight it and if they continue to fight it despite increasing pressure from the company, they are in effect, firing themselves.

The key learning for me out of that beginning in management is to not worry about being liked – help people succeed and the rest will take care of itself. Part of helping them succeed is telling them bluntly when they are doing things that will get in the way of their success. If you do it from a place of "I want you to succeed and here is what I think you need to do", that works much better than if you are just telling them what they are doing wrong or should be doing differently and they think you are just trying to be negative.

Another part of giving impactful feedback is tying it to the organizational goals so that it does not appear at all personal. An example of that might be "Our team's goals this year are to improve our sales by 10%. I have counted on your customers to improve by 8% as part of that. If we accept anything less than that, we will miss our team's overall targets, and I am sure you can see how we cannot accept that."

The second big lesson coming from my Neilson/Cadbury years started with me almost losing my job. It was later in my tenure there, and I probably had grown a bit of an ego – after all, I was young, successful, had been promoted several times, and being totally honest, it probably went to my head a bit. I was more interested in telling people what I thought and convincing them that I was right than in hearing what they thought.

One day, I was called in by my manager and his manager. I was told that this was a turning point for me. I either had to change my ways, or I would find myself out of work very soon. They were trying to tell me that I was not very good at listening to and therefore getting along with people. People didn't want to deal with me because I was headstrong and stubborn, and only wanted things to be my way.

I was shocked. At this point, I had been promoted 3 times in 6 years at Neilson Cadbury. I felt I was riding high in my career and didn't understand these two trying to take me down. My first reaction to hearing their criticisms was utter rage!! It was on a Friday, and I went home that weekend and barely slept a wink. I was so angry. I didn't know what I was going to do with that rage, but it was very real, and very raw.

On Sunday afternoon, as I considered going back to work on Monday, a nagging voice started to try and get my attention. It was my own voice. At first, it wasn't very loud, but within a few hours, it became almost a bullhorn. That voice was saying "What if they are right!!??". I kept stewing over that because if they were, that undercut every self-narrative I had going at the time. If they were right, I was not the hero I thought I was with the career on the rise. I was an arrogant asshole about to be fired.

The "what if they are right" moment became a critical moment of discovery for me. That changes things entirely. I could still allow myself the possibility of being that hero I thought I was, and yet still allow for the possibility that they may be right. If there was even a microscopic chance they were right, that dictated a different action than going to work on Monday and giving them a piece of my mind. If there was even a chance they were right, then maybe what I should do is give their point of view the benefit of the doubt and assume they are right. If they were right and people really did view me the way they said others did, I surely wouldn't like that and would do something about it. I think most people who were convinced that they were an arrogant asshole that people didn't like to deal with would try to change that. That is where I ended up – I decided that it didn't matter who was right. I was going to assume there was a chance they were right and therefore take action to stop being "that guy". I worked very hard to show people a different me and, holy smokes, did it ever work fast! One Individual in Marketing had been a large factor in driving my Managers to confront me. He was vinegar to my oil – we could barely sit in the same room together. I thought he was insensitive to our jobs in sales, and I am sure he thought the same or worse of me. (He was in Marketing) To his credit, once I had accepted that maybe I should try to change the way I was interacting with people, he was the first one not more than 3 months later to go back to my Managers and say "Wow, what a change in Frank, Thank you guys for confronting him like that". Derrick Jones – I never got the chance to thank you for that, but now I can say – Thank you for that!!

So there was valuable lesson #2 from the Neilson/Cadbury days – don't let ego get in the way of you accepting criticism. Ego can be a terrible obstacle to learning. It doesn't matter whether you agree or not, if someone feels that way, accept that there is a chance they are right and then take action accordingly. I had no way to lose once I accepted that. If they were wrong, I still came out ahead because I had put work in to become a better person to work with. If they were right, I fixed a potentially career-threatening problem. Either way, I came out of this a much better person! The only possible wrong way to handle this was to let Ego get in the way and say to me, "They are all wrong, don't change a thing". To Mike Maccarone and John Knox – thank you for confronting my behaviour and forcing the change.

Ego can also be used in a reverse fashion. I have met many people in my 43 years whose ego is so strong that they feel they have all the right answers. They can be difficult to deal with and I have seen many people struggle to deal with these types of people as they are constantly fighting to break through the ego and help that person see that they don't have the answers. However, there were many cases in my career where it was a better choice to just go along with the ego and use it to my own advantage. The most frequent occurrence came with customers. Customers were usually in a position where they could help me achieve my company goals. When I ran into a customer who had what I call "the Ego issue", it was very easy to turn that into an advantage. Usually, it just meant going along with their ideas which were often not the best idea, but what I traded for in quality of idea, I gained back in enthusiasm for support. The egotist was always very good at driving their ideas so there were many times where I kept my mouth shut to a degree, and let the egotist take their ideas with my company's products and drive them to success. This not only helped achieve numbers, but it also helped cement relationships. This is a worthy concept to consider with people even within your own organization. There are some people you will never convince that they should consider other points of view, so use that to help yourself rather than fight it and hurt yourself.

In closing, the Neilson/Cadbury years were very good for learning, and for career advancement so overall it was a great experience – and for those who know Crispy Crunch chocolate bars, nothing compares to getting one fresh off the production line!!

Company #3 Nivel Inc

I made the decision to leave Neilson/Cadbury in early 1993. At the time, I was making about $62,000/year there, and I had an offer to go to a company called Nivel for a $75,000 salary. The money was an attraction for sure. There was another factor at play as well. I had heard from my Manager at Neilson/Cadbury that I was about to be promoted to Assistant Director of Sales. This would have been a huge promotion – we had a sales group of nearly 200 people, and I would be 2nd in command! There was one big problem though – I did not think I would work well with the incumbent Director of Sales. I knew if I worked for him, it would not have ended well and it likely would not have started well as I had some real differences with him in how we saw things. In hindsight, it might have been a stupid move – maybe the company was putting me in place as bench strength to eventually take his position. It is a possibility. However, if that were true, I will say that a previous Director of Sales whom I was quite close to, gave me a window into his job and I really doubted I could do the job. His "to-do" lists were ridiculously long, his hours were crazy long and, in all candidness, inside of me there was a voice saying "If you get that job, it will require you to be organized and you know you are not so everyone will finally see the fraud that you are". Yes…that conversation in my mind took place many times! These were all factors which again belied my early instincts of "money and promotion" as being the two most important factors in career decisions. I realised now that comfort in both my ability to do the job, and the people I would be working closely with were also important factors in career decisions. I could have the greatest job in the world but if I was not capable of producing what the job required, my success would be short-lived in that position.

The Nivel position was a good one – Ontario(Ontario is Canada's largest province) Sales Manager (I was reporting to the Ontario Sales Manager in Neilson/Cadbury). I had concerns about the type of company it was as it was a step down from the **calibre** of Kellogg's or Neilson/Cadbury. Nivel was a privately held company out of Montreal that was owned by two gentlemen who were career entrepreneurs.

Here is the unique part of Nivel. I was hired because the sales force at Nivel had just gone through the process of unionising themselves. I was brought in as the guy with the "professional pedigree" to help the company rid themselves of a union. Who had ever heard of a unionised sales force?? I must say, I had never heard of it before and have never heard of it since. It truly was a unique challenge.

What made it most challenging was the loss of trust between the sales force and the company. The owners felt deeply hurt by the move of the sales force to unionise as many of the employees were long-term employees. There definitely was a sense of "**How** could you do this to us".

On the other hand, feelings were just as deep if not deeper amongst the sales force. I have never encountered to this day a sales force that worked harder than that Nivel team. They were not the most polished, but they certainly worked the hardest of any group I have ever seen. In the previous year, the feeling was that they had

had a great year and hit their targets. As such, they were looking forward to great bonuses based on their bonus plan. I never did get into the details with anyone, but the company had a different perspective. As a result, bonuses paid were significantly less than were counted on. That caused a near revolt and thus, a union was brought in.

One of the things I found the funniest about all of this was that our Sales Force was represented by the Steelworkers Union. When it came time at one point to discipline a sales rep, I had to sit down with a shop steward from the Steelworkers union. There are always times in your career where you may question your career choices – believe me, sitting in front of a Steelworkers shop steward to discuss discipline for an employee was one of mine!!

My role was to present employees with a clear choice....do you want to have a career as just a physical worker (there was a lot of physical labour in the Nivel sales position as they actually put product on the hooks in the stores they sold to) and keep the union or do you want to become professionals who will have career potential?

The approach was that by bringing me in, they were going to tap into the training I had acquired from my previous companies and develop the type of people who don't want to be part of a union. Combining that with the owners' willingness to spend money to get rid of the people who wanted the union around, and before long, they would be back in a position where they could run their company without having to answer to any union.

It worked exceedingly well. Within 18 months we were well on our way to a union-free company with an "eager to learn and develop" sales force. Many of the union guys had been pretty much paid to "go away". We spent a lot of our owner's money to make these guys go away but it was totally worth it to my two Managers (the co-owners) as they didn't like answering to anyone – much less the Steelworkers Union! Many of the people who left received big payoffs the likes of which they probably never saw again so it worked out well for both sides.

We were well on our way to our goal. It was late 1994, and if all went well, in the calendar year of 1995, we would have our hearing to de-unionise, and because of all the changes we had made, we were confident that the sales force would vote out the union.

I was feeling good about wrapping up the year late in December. Sales were good, the union was on its way out, and we had a great young, developing, team. **Before the** Christmas break, one of the promising young managers based in London, Ontario, called me. He was passing through Toronto on his way to Eastern Ontario for the holidays with his girlfriend and wanted to know if I wanted him to stop on the way by to have lunch together. I was thrilled; I liked him very much and because he was several hours away, I did not get to see him much. I had met his girlfriend as well, and she seemed very sweet and well-matched for him. They were just a wonderful young couple. We had lunch and had a wonderful time.

Two days later, I received a phone call that hit me like a ton of bricks. Over the holidays, 4 people had been snowmobiling in Eastern

Ontario and had gone under the ice. 3 of the 4 had passed away, and this couple I had had lunch with two days earlier were amongst the 3. I had never experienced anything like that: I was lost for a few days. Nothing else seemed to matter, and my mind was really messed up over this. The funeral was scheduled for early in January.

On the day of the funeral, I received a strange message from my manager at the time. He wanted to meet with me the day after the funeral at 4 pm in his office. This was strange because we were an early morning company – definitely not a late afternoon meeting type of company. We were at our desks by 6 am, and most days, you could roll a bowling ball through our office at 4 pm and have no risk of hitting anybody. We also didn't usually schedule individual meetings – if he wanted me, he came to see me and vice versa. This meeting stewed in my mind, and I phoned my wife mid-morning the day after the funeral and said, "I think I am going to get fired this afternoon". She was, of course, shocked – neither one of us was used to failure, and getting fired is pretty high up on the list of things considered a failure. It certainly was not in our career plans!

I attended the funeral, and to this day, it is one of the more heartbreaking events I have ever been to. He could have survived if not for the fact that his girlfriend went under first and he died trying to find her. It was no surprise to me – that was the kind of guy he was. At such young ages; what a terrible loss.

4 pm the day after the funeral could not come fast enough. When it arrived, I nervously went up to

see my Manager, and sure enough, my instincts were right. For the very first time in my life, I was fired. He said very little other than "Thank you for all you have done; we feel it is time to move in another direction. Here is an envelope with an offer for you to consider". Actually, I was very grateful I saw it coming because it would have knocked me over if I **hadn't.** Ultimately, it ended with me receiving a 5-month package from a company I worked at for 20 months. It was an extremely generous package because I had a good lawyer. He made it clear that his position was that they lured me away from Neilson/Cadbury (they came after me, I was not looking), and as such, they would also be responsible for my time at Neilson/Cadbury. In essence, rather than firing a 20-month employee, his position was that they were firing a 20-month + 7-year employee. Given that they paid me well, I had no hard feelings and started focusing on my next steps.

Company #4 – Retail Solutions

Experiencing a job termination is, in a strange way, something everyone should go through just once. It was terrifying!! I had two young children at home, 3 and 5 years old. We were a one-income family, so I was it. While I did receive a decent severance from Nivel, it was only 5 months before that would run out, and no income would be coming to us. Believe me when I say, it does not leave you at any time of the day or night – it is always on your mind, no matter what you are doing. The most surreal thing about going through a job termination was looking out the window at all these cars in the morning, rushing off to work, and you have nowhere to go. It makes you feel like everyone else is invited to the party, but your invitation got lost in the mail.

The first significant thing I did after this experience seems a bit disingenuous. At a time when I should have been saving money, I decided to spend money on a new computer system. At that time, personal computers were just starting to be a "thing," and I thought that while I had some downtime, it would probably be put to good use if I spent some time trying to teach myself how to use one of these new devices. My first computer came with Windows 3.1, and I installed the Microsoft Office program from floppy disks, so I was equipped to explore the wonders of this new world. In hindsight, I would say that investing time in learning the personal computer world was probably a pretty good idea, given how much a part of our lives they have become.

I was struggling with the direction of my career, however. I did not want to go back into a traditional company like I had been. The problem comes back to my own self-talk telling me that I didn't fit in. The problem was, my self-talk was right. Whether it was Kellogg's, Neilson's, or any of the myriad big companies out there, the executives in those companies were actors in their roles for the most part. All trying to look the part, all trying to talk the talk, and all trying to compete for that next big promotion or raise. I hated the phoniness of it. I remember one of my Managers at Neilson/Cadbury in a performance appraisal using the phrase "does not suffer fools gladly" when referring to me. He was so right – my tolerance for phonies was about as low as anyone I know.

I kept in touch with a recruiter friend of mine for many years. One day, he suggested speaking with a friend of his who was starting up a new business. This was a gentleman whom I had interviewed with a few years back and quite liked. It turned out, he had recently sold a business for a tidy sum and was looking for something new to do. I met with him, and we hit it off right from the start. We both loved to laugh, were quick to size up situations, didn't sweat the smaller stuff, and were driven to succeed.

His company idea was a "right place, right time" idea as far as I could tell. The time was 1995. This was a time when health food products were really starting to get some mainstream retailer attention. I know it seems hard to believe now because health food products are available everywhere, but back in the 90s, health food products were primarily limited to health food stores. His idea was to work with American companies to bring their health food products into the Canadian mainstream market so that they would be available in mass market retailers such as Loblaws, Walmart and Shoppers Drug Mart. The premise was that the US companies had little to lose – they had both of us to manage their Canadian business, and all they had to do was cash our cheques every month.

We were in the right place at the right time. It was a lot of work for just two guys, but we utilized a lot of 3rd party companies to take care of logistics, billing, marketing, etc. so that we ended up making good use of some "corporate" golf memberships we bought.

We had one problem in the business. About 3-4 days every month, my partner would disappear. Before long, it became clear to me that he had an addiction problem. It was alcohol. As hard as he tried, it became clear to me at one point that I either had to force him to leave the company or I had to leave on my own.

I saw firsthand the devastation this disease had on one of the most incredible personalities I met in my 40 years. He was intelligent, creative, insightful, had a great zest for life, and a wonderful sense of humour. Alcohol took all that away. At first, it wasn't too bad. He would disappear for a day or two, but I held down the fort.

It got much, much worse. I got pulled in by his wife in her frantic efforts to try and save him. We had suicide attempts, we chased him through seedy hotel strips to find his choice of the day, and eventually, it became too much for me.

I had an ethical dilemma to sort out. He founded this company. However, it was clear, he could not run it on his own. He was so far in the depths of the disease that if I weren't there, it would only be a matter of time before serious issues began to get missed on behalf of our large American clients. My choice was, do I make a move to take over the company and maybe move him to a support role rather than the President role he was in. Or, do I just leave? I eventually decided to leave because I just didn't feel right forcing a guy to give up control of a company he founded.

The sad ending to this chapter was that he was not happy I was leaving him. He screwed me out of $5,000 and our friendship was over. Several years later, I heard through the grapevine that he died in his mid-50s. Although we had a somewhat acrimonious breakup, it made me very sad to hear that he had passed. He had so much to give to both the business world and his family of 4 children. On top of that, I have very fond memories of when we did work together – we got along so well we could almost finish each others sentences!

Company 5 – Swenson Canada Inc.

As I pondered the decision of where to go after Retail Solutions, I found myself at a crossroads with two potential career paths. It was one of those pivotal "fork in the road" moments. I was in the process of applying for the position of Ontario Sales Manager at one of the largest bread companies in the country. Simultaneously, I was considering a role with Swenson Canada, the exclusive distributor of Wahl brand hair clippers and trimmers in Canada, offering a National Account Manager position for $57,500 – a step down from my roles at both Nivel and Neilson/Cadbury, both in scope of responsibility and in salary.

Earlier in my career, I naively believed that decisions would be straightforward – if a move advanced my career and increased my income, I'd go for it. At this juncture, I realized it wasn't that simple. The prospect of returning to the corporate rigmarole and the insincerity prevalent in most large companies, like the bread company, made my stomach turn. The thought of surrendering the flexibility I enjoyed working mostly from home for the confinement of a 9-to-5 office routine was equally unappealing. The salary offered by Swenson Canada was less than desirable – a stark contrast to what I had earned at Nivel and Neilson/Cadbury. It was also about $18,000 less than what the bread company was paying.

Yet, something about the Swenson Canada opportunity resonated with me. The company, co-owned by 2 gentlemen, held exclusive rights to the Wahl brand – a name known primarily to my cheapskate English father, who had used Wahl clippers and bowls on our heads for our childhood haircuts rather than pay for a barber to cut our hair. The operational partner at the time was the individual I'd be working with the most, and I genuinely liked him. He was a Scotsman named Scott Fraser. He was intelligent, personable, and radiated authenticity. He was a great athlete who used to play rugby and was a ranked squash player. He told me that all he cared about was growing the business, and while the salary he was offering was less than maybe I was worth, if I did what he thought I could, he would make sure I was

looked after.   Little did I know that I was meeting the person many would later dub my "Brother from Another Mother." Despite being my Manager, he evolved into a true partner in crime and laughter.

The essence of the job was clear – build the Wahl brand within the retail trade, including major players like Walmart, Canadian Tire, Loblaws, Zellers, and prominent drug retailers. It was already a leading brand amongst barbers, but male consumers were now beginning to take a serious interest in grooming so the Wahl brand was well positioned for growth as a Cadillac-type product in the male grooming category. Scott's primary concern was whether I could grow the business, not my adherence to an 8-to-5 office routine. It was so different than the big companies – all he cared about was if I could build the business!!

For me, the decision was both simple and complex. This was a job where I could be myself, without the need to adopt a façade. I knew I could thrive in this role and, more importantly, enjoy my work each day. At this stage in my career, the significance of title and advancement had given way to the importance of finding joy in daily activities. On the flip side, the financial responsibility rested on my wife's shoulders as she looked after the family finances. If I accepted the $57,500 salary, it would undoubtedly strain our household budget. I grappled with a sense of selfishness, knowing that my pursuit of personal job satisfaction would necessitate financial adjustments for my wife and family.

Ultimately, I chose the Swenson job. Despite the negatives and guilt over the low pay, I reasoned that I wouldn't last long at the bread company, putting us back to a similar predicament in a few years. On the contrary, Swenson Canada offered the promise of a fulfilling job where success would be met with rewards. Thus began a nearly 25-year journey with Scott, as we became partners in crime, steering a small Canadian business with 12 employees to become a medium-sized company with 40 employees by my retirement in 2024. The company grew 6x in the time I was there. In 2004, Swenson Canada was purchased by Wahl Clipper Corporation of Sterling, Illinois and in somewhat of an anomaly in corporate buyouts nowadays, Scott and I stayed on with the company. I stayed until 2024, and Scott is still with them. Another great part of this was that Scott was every bit true to his word when he hired me – we were successful, and the reward did follow. So nice to see someone keep their word!!

In hindsight, this was another chance for me to learn that my initial assumptions about career choices were wrong – there was far more to consider than position and money. I have no doubt that the Swenson position was the right position for me, and it led to my being promoted to VP in 2008 and Company President in 2016. What made it right, despite the low pay to start, was the people I would be working with and the nature of the position. I had decided against the bread company because it was the "same old" corporate stuff. I chose the Swenson position because it was simply selling, and I didn't have my inner voices telling me I couldn't do that! Selling was the one thing I knew I was good at! Now that you understand the path my career took, its time to move to some of the lessons and the laughs that occurred along the way!

Career Goals

As we've explored in previous chapters, the pursuit of career goals serves as a guiding force in shaping one's professional journey. In the early chapters, my decisions at Kellogg's and Neilson/Cadbury were primarily driven by financial considerations and the strategic enhancement of my resume. It was a period dedicated to ascending the professional ladder and securing more substantial financial rewards.

As my career progressed, particularly during my transitions to Retail Solutions and Swenson Canada, a shift in priorities became evident. While financial stability and career advancement remained crucial, a new set of considerations emerged, including lifestyle preferences and the allure of a more autonomously supervised work environment, such as the flexibility of working from home.

Reflecting on my career journey, I find contentment with the choices made. Yet, I would encourage viewing one's career through a different lens. Instead of focusing solely on promotions, income, remote work, or job responsibilities, the emphasis should be on control.

Control is the key to influencing the course of your career. For those embarking on their professional journey, the question becomes: How does one attain control? In hindsight, I conceptualize it as starting my career in the backseat of a car, with the company and my Manager occupying the front seat. Unbeknownst to me at the time, what I truly aspired to was to be the one driving that car — the epitome of control.

Control is derived from possessing attributes that the company values. Building relationships with key customers, mastering skills crucial to the business, or possessing unique expertise are pathways to gaining control. Early acquisition of knowledge is a key aspect – the more you learn and the earlier you learn, the greater your chances of possessing skills in high demand.

An essential focus should be

placed on acquiring unique skills. While proficiency in common tools like Excel is valuable, there are many people who have mastered Excel, so you will not stand out in a crowd. Standing out involves learning something distinctive that sets you apart.

When I was with Neilson/Cadbury, my first job was as a Key Account Manager. My job was to sell our products to the major retail accounts. Some of the tools we used involved the ability to say to our customer, "Crispy Crunch has a 12% market share and is #1 in your region so you need to have this chocolate bar because your customers want it". Marketing was the department that provided us with all of the market share data. I personally was quite interested in the market share numbers and I spent a lot of time making myself an expert in those numbers. This made me more confident than most of my colleagues when I was talking with customers for sure, but another side benefit was that my colleagues in the Key Account department started coming to me for answers on market share questions. This became a learning moment about unique skills for me – If you learn a unique skill, your colleagues will begin to use you and your Management will begin to see you as someone others go to

83

for answers – a leader! Until your management sees you as a leader, you will never get the leadership role you desire.

Control empowers the ability to shape our professional narratives, and learning becomes the linchpin to achieving that control.

The earlier you acquire unique skills, the greater control you wield over your career trajectory.

In the subsequent pages, I will delve into instances where the acquisition of unique skills played a pivotal role in taking charge of my career.

Learning As Compound Interest

I previously shared the advice from my father-in-law emphasizing the importance of staying with a company for five years to kickstart a career. However, another pivotal lesson, one that became a cornerstone shaping my behavior over the next four decades, unfolded during my time at Kellogg's.

On a particular training day, I found myself at odds with the prospect of sitting through what I perceived as another mundane session. As we gathered, I couldn't shake the thought, "Another day wasted; they could've wrapped this up in 15 minutes." After lunch, a guest speaker took the stage, none other than Zig Ziglar, a renowned figure in motivation. Surprisingly, I had no idea about his stature; I assumed he was simply there to fill time and make the executives look like they were doing something worthwhile (Yes, I was quite cynical even then about corporate mindsets).

I tried to find a way to keep my interest during his talk so I said to myself "just try to find one thing from what he says that might help you going forward". That change of mindset allowed me to "not miss" one of the most important pieces of advice I received in my entire 43-year career. During his talk, Ziglar said, "You can have everything you want in life if you will just help others get what they want." It hit me like a ton of bricks. The notion that assisting others could directly benefit me seemed almost too good to be true. Yet, it turned out to be a transformative philosophy that became a guiding principle in my life.

Now, I'm not proposing a purely transactional approach. There are instances where you extend help, and people may not reciprocate. That's perfectly fine—no hard feelings. My commitment to this philosophy persisted because, more often than not, kindness begets kindness. Positive energy has a remarkable way of finding its way back, whether through others speaking highly of you or unexpected favors returned.

Another significant aspect is the personal satisfaction it brings. Observing some of my more self-centred colleagues throughout my career, I felt an inner contentment that I was "above the battle." I didn't need to vie for small wins; I had the assurance that treating people well was the best long-term strategy—for both them and **me**. To this day, I am amazed at the importance people place on winning the small battles, that they do not see the negative effect that it has on winning the big war.

A simple example of putting the battle ahead of the war that occurs frequently is salary negotiations. Some people are like a dog on a bone when it comes to negotiating salary. Depending on the position you are in and the strength you have (Unique and desirable skills), the degree of success you have will vary. Suppose you can force your company to pay you more than they want to. There will almost undoubtedly be some resentment depending on how much more they **have** to pay. You may get that extra $5,000, but you may create a situation where your Manager now feels your standard of performance should be higher. Think about it – if they thought your previously lower salary was worth what they were paying you, what do you think they think $5,000 more is worth? Surely, they don't expect the same level of performance that you were giving before. After all, if your previous standard of performance was worth what you pushed them to pay you, they would have gladly done it before. Now you have created a situation where the company feels you owe them more, which puts more pressure on you, and maybe that was not what you were intending at all. I never tried to push my Manager to pay me more – I always wanted a Manager who was happy to sign my paycheck. In the odd times when I was not happy with my compensation, I searched for another job, and the market would determine if I was right or the company was right. If I was right, there should be other jobs available to me at a higher salary and vice versa if the company was right. The key point here is to help your Manager get what he or she wants, and you will get what you want faster. It doesn't work with every Manager, but more often than not, it will work, and you will be ahead in the long run.

If we take the right approach to our careers, we will often be able to help others. I have had many times people want advice on how to talk to the Manager about a particular issue. I will always do my best to give them impactful advice – sometimes it works, sometimes it doesn't. When it does work, more often than not, that person is very aware of where they got the advice from. For me, I am happy just to know that I helped them succeed, as I am content inside knowing that they know where it came from. Hell, even if they don't remember where it came from, at least I do! I have seen others in similar situations who just could not stop themselves from saying to either the person they advised, or the Manager that "I told them to do that". What do they accomplish with that? They make themselves look small in my opinion, and insecure. Those are not labels **that one who** wants to be taken seriously as a Manager wants to be known by.

Reflecting on the power of learning, especially learning a **powerful** concept like Zig Ziglar's advice early in my career, I liken it to investing money early, yielding interest year after year. Over 40 years, a small amount of knowledge compounds into a wealth of wisdom similar to the way money earning interests compounds **over** many years. Imagine if I had only learned Zig Ziglar's advice about helping others in the last year of my career. I would have had only that one year to use it and benefit from it. Similar to the concept of compound interest - If I put $100 into my bank account 30 years ago, it would be worth far more than the $100 I put in last year. Learning reacts in the exact same way.

The Super-Power of Career Dynamics

I had a stint in my career where I was responsible for 23 different countries in Asia (more on the Asian experience later), and I encountered invaluable learning experiences. Amidst my travels, I stumbled upon a pivotal revelation during a breakfast in Singapore in 2018. (By the way, the breakfast buffets in Asia are unbelievably good) As I was reading the morning newspaper, a headline in the Singapore Strait Times caught my eye, declaring "The #1 reason people leave their employers." My initial thoughts gravitated towards factors like salary, bad bosses, job location, or even promotions. However, the truth surfaced – the primary reason people leave jobs is rooted in a lack of perceived respect from their employers.

Respect, often overlooked in the myriad of career dynamics, emerged as the critical factor in employee-employer relationships. It forced me to reconsider the common issues – salary disputes, workplace conflicts, demanding bosses, and overwhelming workloads. Delving deeper, I realized these are not merely isolated challenges but manifestations of a company's ability to convey respect or its absence.

Take money, for instance – often a source of discontent. Beyond the tangible impact on our daily lives, the root cause of dissatisfaction often is less about the money itself and more about the respect attached to it. This is especially true in Canada, where the CRA seems to take so much of our hard-earned income!! I have seen people furious over a $3,000 a year discrepancy. Think about it -

$3,000 is less than $300/month, and once the government gets through with it, it is probably less than $200/month. It is almost indiscernible on your paycheck, yet it can still cause huge arguments and hurt feelings. This is usually not because the lack of that $200 is going to hurt someone's life, but is almost always due to the perceived lack of respect, "not getting it" communicates. This insight proved transformative, reshaping my perspective on the dynamics of discontent in the workplace.

Reflecting on times when I felt overworked and disheartened with my company's handling of it, the core issue always circled back to a sense of disrespect. When asked why it bothered me, my response consistently began with, "I don't know how the hell they expect me to do all of this." I am sure there are many of us in a similar position who make similar comments. This comment is entirely focused on how the company thinks about us (the comment focuses on them not respecting our workload). Do they really disrespect us so much that they are happy with us being asked to do the impossible? A little respect from the company or the Manager can go a long way. For example, imagine an employee who feels that way gets called into their Manager's office. The Manager says, "Look, we know things have gotten really heavy for you lately. I wish I could have prevented it, but sometimes you just don't see it coming. I want you to know, I do now see it, and I am working on a solution that I should be able to have in place next week. Can I ask that you just hang on for a few more days? I really appreciate the way you have handled this stressful time". That Manager has shown that employee a world of respect by acknowledging that the employee was not working in a vacuum and not being thought of - the employee was in fact, being thought of and was so valued that the Manager took their valuable time to try and figure out a way to solve the issue. Respect was not just an Aretha Franklin song – in business, it is one of the most powerful tools we have to interact with each other.

The power of respect hits in so many ways. Years ago, I was with Scott who was my Manager at the time, and we met with a buyer from Canadian Tire. I was a National Account Manager at the time. After our meeting, Scott as President, says to the buyer "So, are we treating you okay" which really means, are we handling your business to the standard you expect? Her answer was "Oh yeah, Frank is great, if I have any problems, he responds right away". Now think about that. She didn't say "Frank is smart, Frank is helping us build our business, Frank is innovative, Frank gives great presentations" – all she said is I can respond quickly to an email or a phone call. Why was that the first thing out of her mouth? Look at it through the respect lens – I answer her quickly; it shows her that she is important to me. It means...and here is that word again, I respect her and what she needs.

Response time is one of the most underrated ways of showing respect amongst not only customers, but colleagues. How many people reading this right now have people in their lives who drive them nuts because they don't respond quickly? The people who don't respond quickly are saying to others, "I have more important things to do than to answer your email or 'you don't matter enough to me'". I know there are times when family things come up for sure, or other circumstances, but someone with a track record of lousy response times is someone who very likely is not a respectful person. And before anyone thinks "well he just doesn't understand how busy I am", I went through a period where I ran 23 countries in Asia from Canada, and ran Wahl Canada, and I am proud to say my response time did not suffer regardless of who it was who was requesting something of me. It is not just me – I have worked with Scott for most of my 24 years at Wahl, who is the busiest person I have ever worked with, and he is extremely strong at response time. If you want an organization that has a chance to work well together, response times must be important for your company in my humble opinion.

The worst thing a Manager can do is not give a good response time to their own team. I can't tell you the number of times in my career where I heard "Here I am trying to get their project done, and I can't get a frigging response out of them!!" The Manager in that position might as well say to them, "I don't respect you!!!". Often, it is not the timeline of the project that is bothering the person waiting for the response – it is the lack of respect they are feeling in not getting a timely response. They don't feel properly supported in their efforts. They are busting their ass to get things done by a timeline and their Manager doesn't feel half the urgency they do. And now that we know the importance of respect, is there anything worse you can say to an employee?

I learned to scrutinize respect in every interaction. A telling example unfolded during my tenure at Wahl, where a young marketing executive expressed his belief that he was underpaid. Instead of preparing to refute his claims as would have been my previous instinct, I put my "Respect Glasses" on and viewed the interaction through the respect lens. What this means is that I had two levels of interaction taking place – the actual conversation about the nuts and bolts of compensation, and secondly, my goal of making him feel respected as he went through this process. Listening to his concerns laid the groundwork for him to feel respected. I told him the logic behind our compensation system but also asserted that it 'was not perfect.' As the discussion progressed, I assured him that I would take up his case with Human Resources to identify what their perspective was and why he was being paid what he was. He may not have known this, but this was already half of what he was looking for when he opened the discussion. He felt great that the company President (me) was going to take up his case with HR. This absolutely made him feel listened to and heard. The outcome actually surprised me because I had thought the company had done their homework properly, but HR had in fact made a mistake. The company recognized that and brought his pay up to where it should be. So not only did he leave that interaction feeling respected, he had a bit more cash in his pocket as well. If the company had found out he was being paid properly and therefore had kept his salary where it was, I would argue, he still would have felt better. He would have known why the company felt his pay was where it was, and he would have known that he was not being taken for granted. He may still have disagreed, but at least he would know that the company was trying to do the right thing in "their minds" rather than not caring enough to consider his request.

The lessons I learned about respect taught me to enter that interaction with two goals:

- **Resolve the matter in question** – he was asking for more money
- **Make him feel respected** – Even if the answer had come back that he was paid fairly, he would have been given a thorough explanation of the hows and whys. I learned early on in business that we do not always have to agree, but what IS important is that we hear each other and understand each other. That hearing and understanding often leads to "I respect your

position, but we agree to disagree."

The belated realization of the transformative power of respect became a life-changing "unique skill" for me. If you are early in your career and you want to learn one of those unique skills that are career differentiators, respect is a very good place to start. I would also add that viewing conversations through a respectful lens is not just a business thing. Try it in your personal life, and I think you will be amazed by the results.

Think of a car cutting you off.

Assume it is not one of those dangerous cutoffs where you could be hurt, but just one of those annoying cut-ins we all hate. We get angry and go "would you look at that guy" (and yes, I will use guy because way too often it is one of us that does it). We get angry and tell someone else about it, and eventually cool off. What bothers us? Is it the half-second longer that we are stuck in traffic? Is it that the guy might have hit our car (but really he wouldn't have because we saw him coming and made sure he didn't hit us). Most often, it is because we feel disrespected. "That guy didn't give a damn that I was here, he just cut right in". Or tons of other comments all going to "that guy's" mindset about us, often centering on him not even thinking about us, and only thinking of himself. Not sure if I am right? Ask yourself this then...how would you feel if the guy cut in front of you, and at the next light, got out of his car and said to you "I'm really sorry, my son cut his head open and he is bleeding like crazy and I just want to get him to the hospital as quick as I can". All of a sudden, you feel much better. He has topped up your respect level again, and off you go feeling better about your day.

To close the respect conversation, I look at respect in 3 ways. I think there are 3 ways to characterize respect in the workplace – disrespect, respectful, and proactively respectful. Disrespect is pretty easy to identify – talking over people, not answering emails or returning phone calls or anything that demonstrates that an individual is only thinking of themselves.

Respectful people are polite, easy to deal with, usually, and do what they are supposed to do. For example, a respectful person will usually answer your email or phone call promptly, will usually give you room to speak in meetings, and will try and find mutually agreeable solutions.

Where people truly become great leaders, and great people to deal with, is when they become proactively respectful. Pro-actively respectful people will aggressively think of others' points of view and pro-actively take action. Examples of a proactively respectful person's behaviours would include:

- **Emails:** They will answer emails promptly because they assume you would like an answer quickly. They don't send emails with an "fyi" attached – they look for opportunities to add value to the reader through either time-saving or directed information "You don't need to read this entire email if you don't want to – I am sending it because I noticed in paragraph 3 something I thought you would be very interested in".

They think about others: I had a very good Manager who one day was charged with telling our Canadian employees that we were closing down one of our factories in Europe. He did a very good job of telling them all about the reasons why and was very respectful of the group. He missed the one way to take this from a good job to a great job. That was – he did not think about what the group might be thinking. For sure, the first thing on a group of employees' minds when they hear about a closing in one area of the world is thinking "Uh oh...might this be us one day". He didn't address that concern by assuring them that the Canadian operations will NOT be closing down. That would have been a great example of pro-active respectfulness.

Respect is one of the most powerful forces we have at our disposal either as leaders or employees. Many people feel they are respectful and usually are on the big things. Being respectful on smaller matters can have a greater impact on people than being respectful on larger matters. How you respect people when the spotlight isn't on can often determine how much support you receive from people.

"For a short fat guy, I look pretty good naked."

I spoke in the Introduction about some of the colourful characters I encountered through my career, and one gentleman is certainly in the Top 5!! He's one of the truly good guys I have met in my career. He is of a shorter stature, and I would not call him fat, but he is certainly not thin. Physical description does not do him justice – he has a personality that more than dwarfs his appearance. Always smiling, an extremely friendly and gracious host, and an exuberant personality that is a dominant factor in any room he is in. Oh, and did I mention a laugh that shakes the walls – that's him! Stephen Kay joined Wahl as a National Account Manager. He had previously been in his own business, but it seems one of the companies he worked with had some financial difficulties and put him in a position where he needed to get a steady job to get back on his feet. We were very happy to be in that place.

He was a natural for sales – always exuberant, always ready to please and always ready to have fun. Fun is the part that I will focus on, but there was another side to him. He was driven to succeed like almost nobody I have ever met. He knew what he wanted, and he went for it. He was one of the employees who became a friend, and part of the way he did that was that he was very easy to work with. Some employees are naysayers and have plenty of reasons for why they cannot do something – he was the opposite. His dedication was off the charts, and his "can-do" attitude was extremely impressive. I gave him his own chapter in this book because I want to focus on his fun side. At the time he was with us, I was Vice President of Wahl, having been promoted from National Account Manager as we were growing so quickly. We were still a very small sales and marketing office, though, and we worked very closely. Everybody seemed to know what everybody else was doing.

The timing was after the "heyday" of Blackberry, yet he and I were devoted Blackberry users. We both felt with our chubby fingers that a tactile keyboard was better for us. He lived on his Blackberry, and he had a unique way of typing. He was a two-handed typist, so in order to hammer out an email, he literally had to stop what he was doing, bend over in a bit of a stoop and hammer away at his keyboard. This quickly became a source of amusement for Scott and me. We had never seen anyone like this guy who so constantly had their head stuck into their Blackberry!

(and we were pretty devoted ourselves!) I made an offhand comment one day to Scott "I wonder if he schedules in his daily shit". This wide grin came onto Scott's face, and he immediately called in our Administrator for our IT. He asked her if she could from the cloud, force an entry onto an individual's calendar. She said, "Sure, easy to do". So, we called him into a meeting, and were discussing one of our many business issues. Sure enough, he got an indicator of a message, and while we were talking, he looked at it quickly. His brow furrows, and we could see him thinking it over. We asked him, "Something on your mind?" He says "I just got this weird message on my calendar – "Take shit, wipe ass". Needless to say, after that the meeting was over – I don't think we have ever stopped laughing about that one. He, of course, laughed louder than anyone–he loved it.

Another funny story occurred later and also involved him. The UFC fighting series was planning its first-ever event in Toronto in 2010. At this time, UFC was one of the fastest-growing "up-and-coming" sports. Another colleague and I were talking, and he is a big fan of UFC, so he suggested we look to take a customer to the event so that the three of us and a customer could have a nice dinner, and go see the very first UFC event in Toronto. We invited a customer who was President of a (at that time) small, growing company, and he was happy to accept. We arranged for everyone to have a hotel room near the event so that we could have a drink or two and not have to worry about driving. And the seats we had were outstanding – probably about 8 rows from the ring!

We met up and had a great dinner, and what turned out to be more than one or two drinks and then headed to the Scotiabank Centre in Toronto for the event. We got to the arena around 8:30. Once we got to our seats, about 15 minutes in, my Colleague who was a big UFC fan excused himself to use the washroom. We never saw him again that evening! I found out later he was not feeling well and went back to the hotel. After another half hour or so, Stephen left to use the washroom but came back with some snacks – great big soft pretzels. We were watching the preliminary events – by now it was about 9:15 and the main event doesn't begin until 11:00. I guess the drinks affected our customer a little more than we knew because the next thing we knew, he was breaking off pieces of the pretzel and throwing them into the ring at the fighters!!! We were trying to get him to stop, but by then, it was too late. Security arrived, and despite our pleading and begging and telling the guard that this was an important customer, our customer was kicked out of the arena. We had to go with him, as you cannot desert a customer. We walked him back to the hotel room, and he had clearly had too much to drink, so we took him up to his room and made sure he could safely sleep it off.

After that, Stephen and I retired to the hotel bar for a nightcap. He looks at his watch, it is 9:40 pm and says "its 9:40 pm – a night which we all looked forward to for months is not even halfway done and we have lost two guys, and the other two (us) aren't even at the event but are sitting in a hotel bar an hour and a half before the main event even starts!!". Ah, the best laid plans.......

One day, I was getting ready to make a call to a customer. Part of that ritual was getting presentations and samples organized. We always used a lot of samples as we thought our products spoke for us way better than we could when it came to putting our best foot forward with a customer. We had a quantity of shared suitcases we used to haul samples around as we often travelled to other cities to see customers so what we usually did was load up the suitcase with samples and then put the presentations in one of the front pockets. Our presentations were usually bound with Cerlox bindings. If you don't know what Cerlox is, it is a series of plastic rings that go through the top of the page to keep all the pages together. On this particular day, I had loaded up my samples and was going to put the presentations in the front pocket. Much to my surprise, when I went to put the presentations in, there was something in the front pocket. As I pulled it out, it became clear......it was a pair of worn men's

underwear. Gross!!!!! While I
suppose I could have been mad, I
thought it was very funny and I
knew only one other person was
using that suitcase, so I was able
to very quickly narrow down that it
was very likely Stephen's dirty
drawers I had been forced to look
at. I started thinking about the
myriad ways in which I was going
to (in a fun way) get revenge. I
went to a female colleague once I
had developed my plan to see if I
was being too cruel with my plan.
I always trusted her judgment
better than mine, but she gave me
the green light. I think the turning
point for her was that they were
worn....all bets are off if you make
your colleagues see your dirty
drawers.
The first thing I did was text
Stephen to ask him when he was in
the office next. His response was
quick... "Tomorrow". I said,
"Okay, please come see me when
you come in." This was by design

vague, as I knew it would get him guessing as to what was up because I was usually much more open about things. He came back almost immediately "Okay... anything I can prepare?" – he didn't want to come right out and ask me what was going on. I replied, "No, just come see me, please". He knew this was not like me, so I am sure I got him thinking. When the next day came, he was in my office pretty quickly. I tried my best to put on my pissed off face – I am not very good at it because I don't get pissed off very often, I am pretty easy-going at work. I proceeded to tell him the following story:

"Remember when I told you that I was concerned about Canadian Tire and how they were feeling about our company?" (Canadian Tire was my customer, and I had a couple of weeks earlier expressed to him my concern about some issues there). He said he did remember. Well, I finally got that big meeting I was after. I had several buyers, assistants, and two Vice Presidents in the room and was getting set to start the meeting. I had samples laid out for everyone, had the video screen ready to go, and at the last minute, I pulled the presentations out of the suitcase, and do you know what came out with them?" He said he did not. I asked him to go take a look. (Remember, all of this was delivered with my pissed off face). He went and looked in the pouch, and I could see his shoulders let down. I then said, "I pulled out the presentations, and when I did, your dirty drawers caught on the Cerlox binding and went shooting across the table and landed on the VP's laptop". He started to stammer out an apology, but by then I couldn't keep a straight face any longer and we both had a really good laugh.

A final comment on Stephen. He hosted a party for the Grey Cup (Canada's version of the Super Bowl) one year in a hotel suite. Amidst the activity, there are some risqué jokes and innuendoes being made as often happens when booze is flowing and people are enjoying themselves. I overhear him in a conversation with a few people, including my wife and I heard a comment which best sums him up. In his usual high volume voice, I hear "For a short fat guy, I look pretty good naked" followed by uproarious laughter – and his was the loudest laugh. That was him in a nutshell – one of the truly good characters I have met in my 43-year career. A heart of gold and a personality to match.

"Oh, if only we could see ourselves as others see us'

I talked in an earlier chapter about the first Manager I ever worked for at Kellogg's. He was kind of funny in that he came across as Mr. Stern. I was in fear of him for quite a while before I got to know him. After I got to know him, I realized the initial appearance was meant as a message to not only me, but also his work colleagues. The message was that he was a serious player dedicated at all costs to the success of the corporation. The guy I eventually got to know was opinionated to the extreme, had a great sense of humour, and loved to enjoy life outside of work. Years later, I found out he gave it all up and went south to live on a boat – that was a pretty far cry from "Mr. Stern," whom I first met.

He did say one thing that has stuck with me all these years. That was "if only we could see ourselves as others see us". The phrase sounds kind of benign at first, but there are many times I have gone to it in my career to check my own actions. I can think of the time I described earlier where I was sat down by my bosses at Neilson/Cadbury and told that my colleagues were complaining about how hard to get along with I was. In my mind, I was simply pushing out my knowledge to my colleagues to help us succeed and doing my best to make good use of our time by dismissing ideas or thoughts that were only going to take us off of what I perceived as the right track. Seems pretty noble, right? Wrong – it was disrespectful and uncomfortable for others, regardless of whether it helped us get to the right answers or not. At times like that, I thought, yes, if only I could see myself as others see me. I would have seen that I was a bit of a workplace bully when it came to meeting participants, and there was an arrogance that if I had seen it in others, I would have hated it. I wish I knew that about myself at the time, but it took years and hindsight to figure some of this stuff out.

I have also used that phrase other times – it is no secret that I like to have a drink from time to time, and there are times in my career that I was "over-served". In the early days, it was a part of the culture at both Kellogg's and Neilson/Cadbury – both were still "old boys" clubs to an extent, and drinking at functions was par for the course. My wife has been excellent through the years at pointing out my idiot behaviour at corporate events, and I find myself most times learning that my idea of just having a good time is not always the way others view it. I have been far from perfect, but I think I have learned through the years to try and see myself as others see me. It is potentially as helpful to people as anything else I learned through the years. I just wish I had employed it more often!!!

"Pull my finger"

I don't think I have ever seen any of the so-called business experts discussing the issue of humour in business. When I look back on all of my different roles in 43 years, humour is the one thing that stands out more than anything else when I consider my time at different companies. It was important to my success in many ways. It broke down barriers and created bonds, and many of those bonds were critical to my success. I think it is a skill or attribute that is rarely discussed, and frequently undervalued by the "experts" who are every day telling people how to succeed. Humour was as important to me in my career as any hard skill was because it formed bonds with people.

In the early days, when I was with big companies like Kellogg's and Neilson/Cadbury, while there were

126

laughs "behind the scenes", often in official meetings and events, things were quite uptight. It was almost as if they were taking themselves too seriously. My first real eye-opener about how humour can be a positive force was when I was with Wahl in the early days. I mentioned Scott Fraser, My Manager for much of my time at Wahl. He was/is one of the funniest people you will ever meet. As I watched him, I noticed something. We would go to events such as customer events or corporate events, and because I was always at his side, we seemed to be the "cool kids", the ones everyone wanted to hang around. I couldn't believe that going to customer events and all the important buyers from companies like Wal-Mart, Canadian Tire, and others would want to hang around Scott. Other salespeople gathered round as well, like he was the Pied Piper. It didn't take me long to figure out, it was laughter that was his "secret sauce". All these high-powered executives who put on this serious appearance for public consumption love to let their hair down and have a good laugh. They don't want to hang around uptight people. That was a turning point for me because in many instances in years past, I was told to keep my sense of humour in the background. After watching Scott, I learned that a sense of humour can be front and centre and can be used as a huge asset because most people do not recognize the value of that sense of humour. Scott did recognize it and made it work to his huge advantage. We would go to the Wahl Head office, which is again, a corporate Head Office with all the dignity and stature of a worldwide office, but without the laughter that we were able to have in our little 40-person operation in Canada. Even there, people seemed to gravitate to us because

128

it seemed they just didn't have enough fun in their days. Scott and I found ways to be successful and have fun at the same time. The one watchout I would add to this is to make it "humour without hurt". It is not an asset if your humour comes at the expense of something that someone takes very seriously.

One example of the use of humour with a customer was that as an Account Manager at Wahl one day, I was in a sales call with a customer. This customer had become a pretty good friend. Scott was my Manager at the time and was with me. This customer was a very down to earth type with a great sense of humour and for whatever reason, he decided he was going to give me a hard time (Just for fun!) on every page of my diligently researched PowerPoint presentation. He took it to the extreme, challenging me on things like why my page number was in the bottom right corner instead of the bottom left. Now, in quite a few roles I have had, my Manager would have been the Corporate type who jumped in and tried to help me defend myself. Not this time!!! Scott quickly figured out what was going on and he joined the banter...on the side of the customer!!!!! So, for me, it became more ludicrous by the second...me trying to pretend to be putting forward serious market data while the entire time I had Abbott and Costello playing "Who's on first" with my presentation. (Google Abbott and Costello "who's on first if you don't get the reference.) The presentation ended with the three of us in hysterics, and the customer continued his strong support of our company. The point of this is that years later, I can bring up that day with either of them, and we instantly have a bond to share.

Conversely, when I was an Account Manager at Neilson/Cadbury, we had a big problem with A&P, a major grocery retailer at the time. As a member of a company owned by Weston Foods, who also owned Loblaws, A&P at the time had decided they were not going to buy anything from the competition and therefore most companies owned by Weston Foods sold nothing to A&P. I had a great Manager who supported me in my attempts to break down that door and we eventually did. That was a major breakthrough! I mentioned in an earlier chapter going to a sales call with my Manager, and having a great call with the customer. When we came back out, the only thing my uptight Manager wanted to talk about was that we laughed too much in the call and it wasn't Professional enough for him. The buyer was probably laughing the most, so I am pretty sure she enjoyed her time in the call. That difference in approach between this Manager and Scott helps to explain why I was so uncomfortable in the big company environment of Cadbury and so "at home" with Wahl.

One day I was in a meeting at Cadbury. We had about ten people in the room and the door was open. Mid-discussion, this loud buzzing was heard from the doorway and in flew the biggest fly I had ever seen. He was slow-moving and flew just over "head-height" down the entire length of our table which totally disrupted the meeting as we all stared at this marvel. While I was thinking to myself "how did he even get off the ground" because of his large girth, our Director of Marketing at the time Norm Williams said for all to hear "I have never seen one with testicles before". That's one way to add laughter to a boring stuffy meeting!!!

We used to have to attend what were known as Home Hardware meetings. Home Hardware is one of the big hardware retailers in Canada with over 1,000 stores. Twice a year, they bring everyone into St. Jacobs Ontario, their warehouse to put on a product display for all of their store Managers/Owners. These shows begin on a Sunday morning and run through a Tuesday at 6pm. Industry-wide, these are known as some of the most boring functions we have to attend. Twice a year we have to stand in front of our booth for 8-10 hours a day with very little traffic as the warehouse is huge and not every store sees every supplier. The result is that you get suppliers standing around talking to each other and watching the time more than they do anything else. One year, our booth was on the aisle adjacent to the main aisle that most people went through. This was nice – I was finally going to be in a busy area. Little did I know how much I would enjoy this show. Early on Sunday morning, this odd little man from the booth next door called me over and says "watch this" and pointed me towards the main aisle. I had no idea what he wanted me to watch but as I was watching the main aisle with all these people walking by this very obvious loud fart noise went off. My odd little man had a fart machine with him!! More and more he was spreading the word so we ended up spending three days with about 10 of us (yes, ladies too!) watching people react to the noises as they walked by. The most notable reaction was an old couple who walked by. She was short, probably under 5 feet, with gray hair and was reasonably heavyset. He was also rather heavyset, but significantly taller.

They walked by and my new friend hit the button. The woman did not miss a beat – she was on his left side and her right wrist was like a cobra striking as she backhanded him in the gut. He turned and looked at her like "It wasn't me!!!" but the damage was done – we were all unsuccessful at hiding our laughter. Yes Canada, this is Corporate Canada hard at work!

Mistakes were often a source of humour. I don't think I could have enjoyed mistakes as much in big companies as I did with Wahl. We had a lady who worked for us in the Marketing Department. She was a perfectionist and very, very, good at her job. She was responsible for proofreading so was an extremely detailed individual. We had an expression which was kind of a brand slogan at Wahl – The Brand used by Professionals. This came about because Wahl started with Barbers and was still the leading barber brand so it helped us communicate to the consumer that we were "the good stuff". One day we were told to check out one of our packages – there might be a mistake on it. So Scott and I looked and found the error discussed. In English – it said Wahl – the Brand used by Professionals. In French, and I will not quote the French but the translation came out something like this – Wahl – Guide for Your Right Ear. I know many companies where heads would roll over this. Scott and I could not stop laughing over that one. No big deal, just fix it in the next run. We knew we had someone very good doing our packaging and somehow this one just got by her – nothing to worry about and besides, we got a good laugh out of it.

Scott and I were at Walmart one day and they requested that we develop a small animal brush. The buyer had a daughter that liked brushing her hamster and we had many brushes for dogs and cats so why not hamsters? We decided that positioning the brush as just for hamsters was too small a market so expanded it to a small animal brush. We gave the assignment to our Marketing Assistant who went away to dutifully design a backer card for a brush for small animals. She came into my office to show me the card she developed. It had a hamster, guinea pig and rabbit on the card. The hamster was on the bottom, the guinea pig in the middle and the rabbit behind. The only problem was that the rabbit had what looked like a bit of smile on his face and he appeared as if he might be humping the guinea pig. I laughed a lot when I saw it. My innocent Marketing Manager did not see it until I pointed it out. She still doubted me so I called

Scott in and asked him what he saw and he just started laughing – he saw what I did. We did redesign the card and launch a more suitable product.

As a final thought, the most successful business relationship (Scott) I had in 43 years was built on the bedrock of humour. We used to talk all the time about some of the high-powered meetings we attended (or didn't attend for that matter) and wonder to each other if those meetings couldn't use a good dose of someone right in the middle of the meeting saying "pull my finger". Additionally, I found that being successful with customers was very closely linked to those who had a sense of humour. I struggled with the uptight "just business" clientele because humour was my "go to" and without it, I was lost. I did find, however, that bonds were very strong when they were established over mutual humour. My thinking is that many corporate cultures could use a good dose of a bit more humour. I have seen way too many employees and even customers say that the place they work lacks fun – what is wrong with adding fun to a workplace?

Quality above everything else....except our jobs!!!

I remember early on in my Neilson/Cadbury days, we had some great and some 'not so great' leaders. One of the things you often hear from leaders in the food business is "we have to put quality above everything else". "Freshness matters, and we will do nothing to compromise getting the best possible products we can to our customers". I remember shopping the produce section at Metro (a large Canadian grocery chain) during the time that their advertising kept pushing that they were "fresh obsessed". You would not have seen some of the garbage I saw in their produce section if they were truly "fresh-obsessed".

It is hypocrisy like this that used to drive me nuts. When I tried to fight it, I was inevitably told that "yes, quality is important, but we still have to get results". I would always leave that conversation thinking to myself, "longer term, if the best quality product is important to results, then why are we compromising to hit a short-term result?". I will give you an example I saw many times with Neilson/Cadbury. (I am not picking on them; from what I knew at the time, a vast majority of food companies operated the same way.) The example is this – it is year-end, mid-December, and it looks like we will fall short of where we said we would finish this year. That doesn't have to happen, though. We can go to our largest customers and offer them a deal to bring in significant quantities before year-end, so we can make our results, and they (the customers) can get a deal. Everyone's happy, right? Wrong – the one group in this equation who will not be happy is the consumer.

The customer has brought in maybe 1-2 months of extra stock, meaning that there eventually will be stock on the shelves that is 1-2 months older than it should be. Unless you are selling something like hammers, this should be a concern. It should especially be a concern to food companies that spend 11.5 months of the year preaching about freshness and quality, meaning "everything," and expect you to forget that in the last half of December. It not only makes the company look insecure and desperate, but to the salespeople representing the company, it does not give them a sense of pride either. It also makes hypocrites of the Senior Leaders in the company. I remember one time saying to a customer how much Cadbury values quality and freshness and her response was 'unless you need to make the numbers'. I couldn't argue with her and I resented being put in that position by my company.

I drove many of my Managers crazy in various ways because of this type of thing – I bristle at hypocrisy and did my best to make sure I was not a part of it, or if I was made to be a part of it, to make it clear to everyone around that I was "onto" what they were doing. Another area that I differed greatly with corporate cultures was the long-term point of view versus the short-term point of view. An example of this would be sales targets.

I often heard from Managers playing their parts as hard-drivers that we "have no option – we must hit this target". I always wanted to say "what happens if we don't," but it was pretty clear by the tone and things that were said that the world was pretty much coming to an end as we knew it if we were to

143

miss that target. Sometimes we would hit that target and they would go away and pat themselves on the back as good "results- oriented" Managers who sometimes have to "crack the whip".

Inevitably, there were times when we missed the target. You might ask, "Well what happened then?" Almost without exception, nothing happened. The company didn't fold, people were not fired, and I was still able to get up in the morning, have my breakfast and head to work. This bred in me a learning that to get too uptight over the targets of the day was just the wrong approach.

My approach from the very early days was to ensure that I and my various teams were doing the best we could possibly do to achieve maximum success for the company. This is where I drove managers crazy. If we were having a tough month, as happens to even the best companies, I would attend the frantic meetings called by Managers who wanted to be seen to be concerned about less-than-stellar numbers. In those meetings, the tone was always grave, and there was this implied urgency that we needed to figure out what the hell to do because whatever we were doing was not giving us the results that we wanted. I often failed to have the urgency required because I knew that I was already doing all that I could to succeed, as was my team, and just because results were not what we wanted, does not mean that I should change my approach or our team's approach. If you are doing the best you can, there is not a whole lot you can, or should change! Panicked meetings, short-term strategies, and desperation, all designed to hit one target never do anything to help the long-term success of an organization. Yet it seems those types of meetings take place all too frequently in too many companies even nowadays.

Another way I am sure I drove Managers crazy was that in many corporate cultures, in order to play the game properly, you have to appear to have every answer, know every number, and never be flustered. I used to have Managers who got pissed at me for not knowing the exact dollar amount my territory was at for the month. "How can you run your business without knowing exactly where you are at all times?" The answer is easy – I can run my business very successfully without tying myself to a spreadsheet and instead devoting my time to ensuring that my team and I are doing all we can to succeed. Again, if we are doing that, the results will be, what the results will be. They may not always be

what the company wants, but my
mindset was always, the company
needs to accept my results as the
fruits of our team doing all we can
– if they don't like the results, they
know what their options are.
Needless to say, while I got along
well with many of my Managers,
this aspect of my personality at
one time or another grated on all
of them.

Are we making enough money?

Most of my career was spent on
the sales side of the business, and
the selling was almost always to
large retailers. Throughout those
43 years, there was a lot that went
into trying to be successful at
selling products to retailers. It

seems simple to figure out how to motivate a retailer to buy your product – give them a proposition that shows them how your product will help them make money....right? Well, yes and no. Retailers are for sure dominated by discussions about how to make more money, as are most companies. Where things become a bit more complicated is when a retailer tries to consider how a proposal might make them the most money. There are many factors that they have to take into account:

- Profit and Sales dollars
- Gross Profit Margin percentage
- Inventory

There are many more, but those are just a few. Suppose we sold a retailer a product that cost them $80, but they resold it for $100 retail. Their profit on this item is $20 or 20% Gross Profit margin. If they sold 100 of these items in a year, their gross profit on the item would be $2000. However, if it came in a case pack of 20 per box, this would cause additional questions. To buy one case would cost them $1600 or 80% of their annual profit. Add in interest rates, and how many stores would be selling the product, and you can easily see how inventory requirements are also an issue to be considered when it comes to convincing retailers to buy your products.

In my early years, I spent a lot of time having to get proposals approved before I could take them to a customer. Invariably, the first question on every manager's mind when I brought in a proposal was

"Are we making enough money?". This seems like the right question to be asked, and if it is asked often enough, you probably have a successful company, right? I am not here to argue with it, but I have experience with a different philosophy that seemed to work very well.

When I went to work at Wahl, as I have said before, Scott was my Manager. In the early days, before we were bought by Wahl Clipper USA, Scott was a 50-50 partner in the company, so he had more on the line than any of my previous Managers when it came to ensuring that the company was making enough money on our proposals. You might expect that he would take "are we making enough money" to another level, given that it was **his own**

money!! It might surprise you to know that he went almost in the opposite direction. His question always revolved around whether the proposal made enough sense for the retailer to be interested. So there were many times where he put me on the spot to explain why this proposal would work well for Wal-Mart, or Canadian Tire, rather than Wahl Canada.

I was at first stunned, and it felt awkward, but once I fully understood why, I realised how "industry-leading" his outlook was. We could present the most profitable proposal possible for Wahl Canada, and yet, if it didn't do well for the retailer, they would probably not be interested. More importantly, even if we were good enough to get them to take it, sooner or later, a competitor will

come in with a counter proposal –
the less money we made for the
retailer, the easier we made it for
the competition to come in and
"mow our lawn" as we called it. It
made it easy for them to beat our
proposal. Don't get me wrong,
Scott liked making money as much
as anyone I ever worked with, but
he was thinking way beyond just
"get the product on their shelves",
he was thinking "I want it on their
shelves and I want it to be next to
impossible for a competitor to take
us out. I can think of a couple of
examples at a major Canadian
retailer where we did such a good
job in 2002 of making something
work for the retailer that, as of
today in early 2025, they are still
carrying two products we listed in
2002 because we made the
economics so good for them. It

was good for us, too, but it was next to impossible for a competitor to beat us. It was this philosophy that took us from a last-place market share of less than 5% in 2000 to approximately 70% and market-dominating when I left the business in 2024. My experience is that too many businesses live day to day and few take a long- term outlook. As you can see, I am a big believer in the long-term outlook. It made my job easy for many years!!

Watch people and they will show you who they are.....

The expression "watch people and they will show you who they are" is a common one amongst Managers in business because let's face it, Managers are in the people-observing business. Whether it is before hiring, after hiring, or dealing with customers, you better be able to read people well or you will have no success in creating a team that will give their all to make you successful as a Manager.

Many people talk a good game, but you would be surprised how many do not "walk the walk". Some of the expressions we hear from Managers all the time are:

☐People are our most important assets

☐Supportive environment
☐Respectful environment
☐Family-like atmosphere

Unfortunately, my experience is that the ideal representation of those wonderful aspects listed above rarely, if ever, exists. There are two main reasons for this, I find:

☐Managers are not equipped to know how to do this
☐Managers do not fully embrace these principles as frequently, their own career needs come first.

Managers who are "not equipped" frequently have good intentions but just do not realize the impact of either their words or actions. Think about either yourself or others you know – frequently, people place higher priorities on things because "the Boss needs/wants this". Or maybe you have heard someone who got a compliment from a Boss – compliments from Bosses frequently get repeated to friends/family. It also seems to me that negative comments about a person frequently carry a lot of weight with people, and that impact is multiplied exponentially when it comes from a Manager.

Given all that background, which many Managers do not fully comprehend, I have seen so many times where what might normally be termed "minor oversights" have huge impacts on people. Many managers forget to say a simple thank you, which can have a huge impact on an employee. Praising a job well done frequently escapes these types of Managers, but when a job is not done perfectly, nothing gets missed. It's no wonder that sometimes well-intentioned Bosses get a bad name. It takes hard work, attention to little things, and caring for people to be able to effectively manage.

On the other side (and worse) are those that preach a good game for the masses but have no interest in following through on the hard parts of being a good Manager. I can think of one example in particular in my life that stands out the most and truly showed me who a person was. I will not mention any names, but it happened when my wife had an ectopic pregnancy during my time at Neilson/Cadbury. Naturally, all the people at work were truly and

157

sincerely supportive and caring. We received a very nice bouquet of flowers at home shortly after the event. In a discussion a few days later, I was telling my Manager how much we appreciated him sending us flowers and especially noted how much it helped lift my wife's spirits. He smiled, winked and said, "Hey, don't think there isn't a method to my madness, we might need you to work late some night". There is so much to be read into that sentence, and it may be tough on the surface because, as a reader, you did not know the man. I read it this way, and I knew him pretty well. He tried to pass it off as a joke because of his smile, but it came out of his mouth so fast, I knew he had been thinking it. As well, this was again his way (he was very insecure) of making himself sound smart. He thought he could not only do something nice, but also come out of it looking to me like a smart guy who plans his every move. He did accomplish some of this – it was clear to me he plans out his moves, but they are planned out to help him and his career. This was proven many times over in my tenure with him as manager, so I know I didn't misread the situation. His big mistake was in trying to accomplish too much with one bouquet of flowers. He wanted to show us he cared, (whether that was for show or not, I don't know, but I have to give the benefit of the doubt and assume he did care) but he took it step further and showed that he thought of things in terms of himself – he saw an opportunity to make himself look good and he never missed in jumping on those. He would probably have been better off if he just settled for letting us know he cared rather than trying to make something bigger.

In all honesty, in my earlier days, I was probably more about myself than I ended up being in my career. I did try to remember that my success was dependent on others, but when you are career-focused in the early days, it is easy to forget that.

ASIA - ("The whole fkn room shook")

In 2002, Scott and I took our first ever trip to Asia. This was part of an annual tradition for many years, and for about 5 years in the 2010s, I was travelling to Asia 5-8 times a year. Thus opened a chapter in my life that I never could have imagined. I went to more than 15 countries in Asia, and to say that it was probably the most unique experience of my lives would be a gigantic understatement.

The trips to Asia began because we had a big supplier in China who wanted us to come to his factory, so we decided to go. We also looped in some touristy type things as well as a trip to a pet show.

From the very beginning, the Scott, myself adventure began.

and Scott's partner Jack Swenson (prior to Wahl buying us in 2004) were in the office one day discussing the concept of the trip when Scott says to Jack, "oh shit, we are going to have to get those shots". Jack and Scott had worked together for a long time, so Jack immediately picked up on it and replied with something like "yeah, that's the only bad part". Naturally, my curiosity was piqued, and after further probing, I was told that we would have to get a shot for certain diseases (which we did), but they told me the shot was "right in my nuts". If that were to happen today, I would go right to my buddy Mr. Google and be able to discern fact from fiction pretty quickly. (Fiction:"You need a shot in the nuts to go to China") Unfortunately, this was 2002, and that concept was only in its I loved these two guys – not who would they mislead me, right? I had a couple of weeks to stew on this, and when the day came, I was sweating bullets. Scott's retelling of his perspective is probably the best "They called Frank in (we did need to get some shots....just not in the nuts), and as he was walking in with the nurse, all I could hear was him saying to the nurse "you will be gentle with me won't you?". I came out to two supposed Senior Executives who were laughing like little kids about how they got that one over on me. I could laugh, too, because my nuts did not have to go through anything like that.

We had one more event before we left. This was our first trip to Asia. This was a big deal. We planned every detail, printed itineraries, had our shots, our passports – everything!! There was nothing that could go wrong! Except.....there was. We showed up at the airport and were waiting in line, and both Jack and Scott got their tickets out. I started looking for mine....and I didn't have one. This probably sounds like ancient history because nowadays, nobody brings a hard copy of a ticket for a flight. I can tell you, back then, you had to have one! Scott and Jack actually had to buy me another ticket so I could travel with them and then chase the refund for the other one once we got back. We had about an hour of sweat where we didn't know if I would be able to go. After it was all sorted out, Scott looks at me, with no anger or resentment, but he says in the most curious way possible, "I am trying to understand how you can arrive for your first trip to Asia without a ticket". I wish I had an explanation for that – more on this type of thing later. Let's just say I am blessed with an ability to do some of the stupidest shit you could ever imagine.

I don't know how to describe all that went on during that first trip to China. I suppose when I came back home to my wife, the first thing I would have told her was about the crowds. It was crowded everywhere! As it was our first time going, we tried to include all kinds of touristy things such as shopping the markets in Hong Kong, going to the Great Wall,

Tiananmen   Square and the Forbidden City.

Scott and I went to one of the Hong Kong Markets. Little did we know that two big white guys who look like they have money draw attention in areas like this. We had a female guide who took us to this area, and when the car came to a stop and we disembarked, it was like we were rock stars. We were mobbed by people sticking things in our faces, trying to sell us stuff. We moved forward to keep up with our guide (who did a really crappy job of keeping the crowds away ☺) and ended up going into this two story building. Naturally, the guide wanted to take us up to the second floor, where we could do some shopping in private, as the crowds were kept away. Unfortunately, on the way up, we realized there was a very little staircase, and lots of people. The "sellers" were all over us, trying to get us to buy before we went into the private area. It was so bad, Scott and I were both considering letting the elbows fly and man-handling our way out of there. We didn't, and all ended well, but it was quite the eye-opener.

We went to the Great Wall of China and it was a snowy day but it wasn't so bad that we couldn't get out and have a look.   It is staggering to see the size of the wall, and the terrain it was built over. I remember standing there thinking to myself at some point, this   was   simply   rugged mountainous   ground   and somebody decided to put this big frigging wall here. Truly amazing. The funny part for us was that we saw a regiment of the Chinese army there – about 20-25 guys. There were having a snowball fight on the wall, laughing and having a blast. That wasn't quite what I expected of my first encounter with the Chinese army!

When we went to see Tiananmen Square and the Forbidden City (they are in very close proximity to each other), it was a very nice day so we were able to take our time. Unfortunately, that was not our style – we looked at the square for about 5 minutes and said "okay, we have seen this, NEXT!". We then went to the Forbidden City which is really a reasonably small building, or so we thought. My most vivid recollection of the Forbidden City is walking around inside, looking at various exhibits and then leaving after 45 minutes only to find out when we were leaving that we had spent the 45 minutes looking at the next-door neighbour to the Forbidden City. We were wandering through some market for 45 minutes thinking we were looking at the historical Forbidden City! After that, we did a quick glance at the Forbidden City and went for a beer and had a few laughs.

One other thing I took away from that first trip was the number of females in China who turn to prostitution. You can't miss it – it was everywhere back then. It made me kind of sad to see, because clearly it was a much more lucrative option for them than the alternative type of work at that time. Women were still nowhere near equal in business in China, so the jobs for them were mostly menial, and low-paying. Contrast that with the foreign money from Americans and Europeans, and a successful prostitute in China could have many riches compared to her local friends who were working for wages equal to about 1/5th of what the job would pay in North America. It definitely made me sad for them, but it also reminded me of how lucky we are in North America.

Those were observations of travelling in Hong Kong and China, and that was most of my exposure to Asia until 2014. In 2014, many things were taking place in my career. I was heading into my last ten years of my career, and I was Vice-President in a job that I was very happy in. I was lucky enough to work with people that I was happy to see most days, and I almost always came to work with a smile on my face. However, as I looked ahead to the end of my career, I knew I wanted to find a way to bump my income significantly 1-2 more times before I hung it all up. I mentioned this to Scott, and while I had pretty much reached the top in our Canadian organization (except for Scott), I knew that he had enriched both his learning and his income by doing things outside of Canada for the company. At that time, he was President of Canada but also running Sales and Marketing in Wahl Germany. I wanted more, so I asked for more. This got me a meeting with Greg Wahl, our worldwide CEO. Greg was one of the most passionate people I've ever met in my 43 years. He was so passionate, we all knew, if you have a meeting with Greg, you have to plan your escape, or you could be in there all morning – he was so passionate he would just get fully engulfed in whatever the topic was, and it was very difficult to stop him. Many of the stories around meetings with Greg involve people racing out of his office when the meeting was over and darting for the bathroom because they had been in there for 4-5 hours. I had one guy once, I sent in for an interview with Greg, and when he was done, I said, "How did it go?". He said to me, "I don't know, I said Hello, and 4 hours later said Goodbye". I know he was exaggerating, but it was a good line, and I knew the point he was making. In my meeting with Greg, I said to him, I really wanted more from the next ten years than just to be VP of Wahl Canada. He knew I had done some work for him in the US previous to this meeting, so I am sure it was not a big surprise. He said, "How do you feel about traveling to Asia?". I replied that it was no big deal to me because I had been doing it for years. Long story short, Greg wanted me to build a consumer business in Asia. Wahl was always a very big brand with Barbers around the world, but we were only big with consumers in certain markets (Canada, US, Australia, UK and a few others). I still remember him saying to me "In the US, we have 350 million people and we do xxx dollars per year with consumers. In Asia, there are 1.3 billion people in the area we are talking about (Southeast Asia,

23 countries) – how much could we do there?" This was like manna from Heaven.   I didn't want to leave Wahl to improve my income nor my experience, so this was a great way to do both and stay with the company.

I latched onto the opportunity like a dog with a bone. I couldn't wait to dive into this new ground and discover how to build a giant consumer business for the company in Asia. Unfortunately, Greg and I were dead wrong thinking that there were bountiful riches to come our way from consumers in Asia. Wahl's primary consumer business is focused on male grooming – haircuts and facial hair.   Several primary factors were working against our consumer success in Asia that we did not know going in:

Cutting hair at home is just not a part of the culture in many areas of Asia. Going for a haircut and pampering yourself IS a big part of the culture. The thinking often is "why would I want to do that at home when I can have someone else do it for me?". Whereas in North America, I remember my cheapskate Father putting the bowl on my head, taking out the Wahl and buzzing my brothers and me to the point that we had nothing left. While it was definitely a part of my personal culture, I would not say I look back on it with fond memories ☺

Facial hair is not common in Asia. Try and sell a beard and moustache trimmer to a 40-

year-old man who physically cannot grow a beard or a moustache – it's one hell of a challenge

🔲The economies vary greatly in Asia.   Places like the Philippines   and   Thailand, haircuts were so inexpensive that   one   could   easily understand nobody wanting to do it at home – even my Dad probably wouldn't have done it if he lived there! Yet places like Singapore, Japan, and Korea had economies more similar to a North American or European economy.

The real eye opener for me was in understanding that one Asian is not another.   I worked in 20+ countries over there and really got to understand that someone from China is not the same as someone from the Philippines, Korea, Japan, or anywhere else. They were all different. As you read this, you might think "well of course not!". Let me tell you, when I first started, my point of view was simply that if there were 4x the people over there, I should be able to do 4x the business we do in North America. My thinking was very simplistic – they all look similar, so they must be similar. In hindsight, I do recognize how idiotic that thinking was, but it truly was the way I was thinking when I started out in Asia. It is as dumb as someone from Asia saying, "Well, an American looks like a Canadian, looks like an Aussie and looks like a Brit, so they must all make decisions based on the same factors". There may be similarities in appearances, and even if some of the ways we view each other, but the business analysis is nowhere near the same in those markets, just as it should not be in Asia.

Thailand has many areas where the income is very low and rural-based. Singapore is one of the most beautiful cities you will ever see, but the income is high, and the professionalism is tremendous. They have purposely designed themselves to be a business hub for Asia and have taken a lot of business from the more traditional business hub of Asia, in Hong Kong. Japan is a trend-setter for Asia, but is rivalled by South Korea which has been very successful in becoming a huge part of the world's economy. Indonesia is somewhere between the high income of Singapore and the low income of Thailand, but it is the sleeping giant of the region. Indonesia has a huge population that wants to become an economic powerhouse within Asia. One country I really enjoyed visiting was Malaysia. It is over 65% Muslim, and the people there are wonderful. I remember my first trip there being driven from the airport in Kuala Lumpur to my hotel and passing some of the lushest greenery I have ever seen. It truly is a beautiful country. Taiwan's workforce is known to be extremely bright and aggressive in their pursuit of success. Many Taiwanese own factories in China because the labour costs are cheaper in China. That may have changed in recent years as Chinese labour costs have risen significantly in the last 10-15 years, which has opened the doors for countries like Vietnam to compete with them for factories and therefore jobs. I have to say something about the Philippines. One thing I learned in my travels is that there are many millions of Filipino women working in other countries. They leave the Philippines to become maids (domestic helpers or DH) in neighbouring countries (Singapore, Hong Kong, Japan, Korea) where the pay is higher than it is back home. They send money home to their families to help them survive. I mention this because there is no group in the world I have more respect for than the DHS from the Philippines – they work very hard, they make very little, and out of what little they make, they send a significant portion home for their families. This is done all the while they are away from their families, and the lucky ones get home once a year or so to see their families. Wow!! The next time you hear someone talk about someone in North America being "selfless", think about that.

The country that surprised me most? Sri Lanka by a long shot! When I first went to Sri Lanka, I didn't know what to expect. My limited exposure in Canada was that I knew there had been a civil war, and there was some group called the Tamils involved, and many of their members came to Canada and were protesting events back home. I did not view that too kindly as my view is that when we arrive in a new country (as my family and I did), you don't go out on the streets and try and tell your new country what they should be doing – you try to adapt and respect the culture of the country that has allowed you to come in. So I was not at all sure what I was in for when I went to Sri Lanka. Well, the civil war had ended, they were trying to rebuild the country, and the businesspeople I met were some of the most professional people I encountered anywhere. Every person, and I mean every single person, impressed me with their graciousness (a trait that exists in most areas of Asia), professionalism, and welcoming and thoughtful manner. Add to that, it is on the ocean, and there are some spectacular areas to visit. I stayed one trip a resort on the ocean near Colombo, the capital of Sri Lanka, and it was fantastic.

The other interesting part of Asia that I discovered was the dynamics between countries. Amongst the people I travelled with, there was a universal resentment of China. I think it stemmed from the fact that the Chinese were everywhere. With a population roughly 3 times the size of the US, it's easy to see how the Chinese could be everywhere. Within various countries where maybe there were Chinese neighbourhoods, or the Chinese controlled much of their business, a natural resentment seemed to fester throughout Asia.

There are rivalries. I mentioned earlier that Singapore and Hong Kong are competing to be both the shipping and business hubs. Korea and Japan competed to be the leading-edge trendsetters. Vietnam and Indonesia competed to pick up factories that decided, for one reason or another, to leave China.

One aspect of Asia I grew to thoroughly enjoy was the weather. Korea and Taiwan are to the north of the countries I was responsible for in Southeast Asia, so they do get winters. The rest of Southeast Asia did not get much of a winter, if at all. For example, I used to love Singapore because it always seemed it was 32 degrees Celsius (90 degrees Fahrenheit) there, no matter what time of year I landed. The low was in the mid-20s (70s Fahrenheit). Similar climates were seen in many countries (Thailand, Indonesia, Philippines), and this made outdoor activities more common than we are used to in most of the four-season North American cities. Outdoor patios were a year-round thing. I loved working hard during the day, but at night relaxing in one of the many outdoor patios and having a beer to unwind. This was another difference in Asia versus North America. In many places, they do not cook at home – they go out for dinner every night. Some of the apartments people live in are so small that they don't really have much of a kitchen. Going out to eat is a major part of one's day in most parts of Asia that I travelled in. There is definitely something to be said of making meals "more of an event". I used to love the Asian buffets for breakfast. They literally had choices in the hundreds and ranged from veggies, to seafood, to all kinds of meats, soups, and finished with a wide variety of dessert choices. I have a fairly narrow range of tastes, but there still was something nice about the fact that if I wanted to venture out of the tried and true, I could.

Another interesting part of travelling to Asia was the business culture. In North America, business is often conducted without any activities outside of the office environment. In Asia, I guess, because you are travelling to their country and not based in their country, they feel more of an obligation. Often, they are grateful that you are coming to their country all the way from North America. As such, they want to take you to dinner, show you different experiences, and most of all, drink with you. It may be changing now, but back when we first started going to Asia, without fail, we had to go out at night and drink. We didn't just have to drink – we had to drink lots! It seemed to us that the mindset of our hosts was always this perception that North Americans don't have any fun unless they get drunk. I don't know if that impression was formed from previous visits from others, or possibly because Asian businessmen seemed to love getting drunk, so they assumed we did. Very fortunately, both Scott and I were not on our first rodeo when it came to drinking, so we often ended the night with a bunch of drunk hosts around us while we were okay.

I could not do all that travelling in Asia and not come back with a bunch of stories. One of the early events that happened to me, which became a harbinger of my life travelling in Asia, occurred on my very first trip by myself. The Asian assignment had just been given to me, so one of the very first things I had to do was understand the Asian retail scene so I would know what we were dealing with. Would we be dealing with a competitive retail landscape like we were in North America, or would we be more of a ground-breaker? Surprisingly to me, it was quite competitive. Big companies we all know, like Phillips and Remington, were there along with a plethora of smaller Asian-owned companies. My first trip was simply to go to countries, walk through some of the major retailers and get a feel for the retail environment in each country. For someone who is not a planner by nature (I find the background work very tedious), I planned every detail of this first trip. I was also very conscientious about the company's expenditures - probably to a fault. What this made me do was design the most insane agenda for a trip anyone I had heard of had ever done. I planned to hit something like 9 countries within about 12 days. While sitting in Canada designing this, the formula seemed easy - spend the morning in stores, in late afternoon, fly to the next country, rinse and repeat. What could possibly go wrong?? The very first day, I found out what could possibly go wrong. I found out that most of the retailers in

Asia are in big malls and that those malls don't open until 11 am. I am normally someone who gets up 5 am-ish, so to wait until 11 am to start my day was like asking a fish to breathe out of water. Even worse, this made it difficult to do what the company was spending thousands of dollars for me to do – visit stores and get the information I needed to draw up our strategy for the market. I somehow managed to get what I needed out of that trip, but one particular moment stands out. On arrival in Seoul, South Korea, I was to be met by a pre-arranged ride at the airport gate. My driver was not there. It was 11 pm, and I knew I had an hour and a half drive to get to my hotel. What now? Well, I did have a phone number, so I called it. The driver told me he had been delayed but would be there in 15 minutes. I walked up to the place where I was supposed to meet him, it was about a 15-minute walk from where I made the call. I was exhausted – it was bad enough for a guy who gets up at 5 am to be up at 11 pm, but add to that the travelling and I was ready for my bed. With about 5 minutes until his arrival, I noticed something – I did not have a passport. Shit!!! I knew that in Asia, they require a passport to let you into the hotels, and I also knew I would need it for the rest of my trip. I had to quickly retrace my steps. I went back to an information booth where I had stopped when I first got off the plane, because I knew I had talked to a guy there, and I figured I must have put it down while talking to him. It wasn't there. I went back to the gate to ask the gate attendant, by this time I was near freaking out! It wasn't at the gate, so they sent someone back onto the plane to check my place – no luck! It was then that I remembered the phone call. I ran back to the phone booth, which was that "15 minute" walk away, and there sitting on top of the payphone was my passport. By this time, it was approaching midnight, and I had to get back to my driver. Fortunately, he was still there, so the rest of that night was without incident. I don't know if it comes through the pages, but I can't describe how much your heart races in that kind of situation.

Another time, I arrived in Sri Lanka for the very first time. I arrived at the hotel at about 1:15 am, and was being picked up the next day by a potential distributor we were considering hiring for Sri Lanka. Wahl was looking for someone to exclusively distribute our products in Sri Lanka – being a worldwide brand had value to the various country distributors we had, so it meant something in a lot of places when we were looking to expand our distribution network. As such, the distributor arranged to take care of my arrangements the minute I got off the plane. He had a driver meet me and deliver me to my hotel. That part of travelling in Asia was pretty nice! As I was getting to bed that night, near 2 am, I went to plug in my phone and a very familiar panic set in – I lost my phone this time!!! It was easy to track the last place I had it – it was in the car coming from the airport.   I therefore began this new relationship by asking my new business colleague to track down my phone from his driver service – a bit of an embarrassing start to the new relationship.

Hong Kong was one of my favourite places to go in Asia. Despite the Chinese takeover in 1999, it was still heavily under British influence.   I could get around in English almost anywhere. One of the most impressive things about Hong Kong is its subway system, called the MTR (Mass Transit Railway). It is so impressive because it is almost always massively crowded, and yet things move extremely efficiently. You can be standing on a full subway platform 15-20 people deep, and you will see trains coming and going seemingly every 30 seconds, and before you know it, you are on a train. One of the other things I liked about Hong Kong was that I could leave my downtown hotel, go to the MTR station (a short walk from the hotel), and check my bag directly to my airline and my flight from the downtown MTR station. After that, all I had to do was ride the MTR to the airport and check in when I got there. At first, I wasn't sure I trusted that after dropping my bag at the MTR, it would actually show up on my flight. However, I must have done it close to 50 times in my life and never had a problem once! It truly is a great system. One day I checked my bag at the MTR, then found my seat on the train, and it was never crowded, so I had room to put my backpack on the seat next to me and had a relaxing trip to the airport. I always got to the airport very early because I usually had lounge access, and I could either get some work done, have a bite, or just relax without having to worry about a tight schedule of making the flight. This one day, I got off the train at the airport and proceeded to the Air Canada check-in. All of the sudden, that old familiar panic set in – no passport!! No!!! I was on my way home after a two-week trip – I was exhausted, and the last thing I wanted to deal with was this. As I mentally retraced my steps, I realized that after I checked my bags at the MTR station, I waited for my train by a counter, and I thought, maybe I put my passport on that counter. The station was a 20-minute trip so going back there was the first thing to do. I went back and it was not there so I went to the counter, they directed me to the lost and found and there was no passport there. I knew I had had it when I checked in so the only other place it could be was left on the train. I went back to the airport where I knew they had a big customer service counter for the MTR. She told me not to worry, each driver checked every seat at the end of their trip so for sure he or she was going to find it. I was less confident. She also said I could have to wait a couple of hours before I heard for sure. That meant missing the flight!!! I did end up missing the flight but that was the least of my worries. As I was waiting for her to get a phone call from the driver, I was researching what happens when you lose a passport abroad. I would have to go first thing Monday morning (this was Saturday) to the Canadian embassy in Hong Kong. After that, it could take up to two weeks to get a replacement. Two weeks! What the hell am I going to do for two weeks in Hong Kong? I was desperately hoping that the driver would find it in his/her checks. Finally, about an hour after my plane left, the lady at the counter gets a phone call. I heard her speaking in Cantonese and at one point I heard "Robert" which is my middle name and I knew they had found it. I guess I had put it on the seat and then put my backpack on it and when I left, I simply took my backpack and left it sitting there. It did cost me an extra night in Hong Kong, but I can tell you, I was so relieved, I think I smiled all night long.

After so many passport mishaps, I was convinced that I needed to do something about this tendency of mine. I bought myself a passport holder which hangs around my neck, and since doing that, I have never misplaced it. It is foolproof, or as my wife would say, "Frankproof."

Those are some of the main "idiot-Frank" stories from my Asian travel days. There are lots more, but I think you get the point – I can easily become preoccupied or distracted and miss the obvious, like "I need a passport to travel".

One of the things I am often asked when I discuss travelling in Asia is "Did they make you eat strange things?" The answer is an unqualified "YES". This is my warning before you go any further. If you are squeamish, skip this section. I am going to talk about some of the stranger things we ate during our travels. In our early years of going over there, one night we were out with a group of people, and they decided to show us the local delicacies. Now, Scott and I, the successful and confident North American business people we were purported to be, were up for the challenge. They took us to a restaurant, and the first thing we had to do was stop with our hosts at the aquariums at the entrance.

There was this huge wall that was nothing but aquariums. Our host literally went from one to the other, picking out various "live" things to be our meal that evening. That evening we ended up eating jellyfish, snake, and if you are squeamish, skip this part....dog. Jellyfish were like a glazed rubber band...chewy with no taste. Snake was more bone than skin with really no taste to it at all. Dog was very rich, but it's hard to really discuss the taste because our minds were elsewhere when trying it. Before anyone wants to jump on me for doing this, understand, it is still quite a common thing in many areas of China. They raise them on farms for the express purpose of selling them as food. However, many people over there are just as put off by the concept as North

Americans are. One of our good friends over there heard we did this and he was disgusted – he kept saying "you were eating your customers!!". (We sold a lot of pet products). To this day, I am not sure if it offended him that we were actually eating dog, or being the businessman that he is, he was offended because we were contributing to something that was taking our customer base lower ☺. In our defense, we were simply trying to be respectful of a host who wanted to show us all about Asian culture. We could have done without that part!!

The original reason Scott and I started travelling to Hong Kong in 2003 was to visit certain factories we bought products from. Once a year, we would go and sit in the company's showroom in the Shenzhen, China factory and would discuss all the products we buy. They would put all the products they sell worldwide out for us to see, and then we would engage in a day-long discussion about what we might be able to take from someone else's success in another country and bring to Canada. It was a very effective way to ensure that we stayed on top of worldwide trends in certain categories. In one particular factory, we would go with the factories US agent, and he would help liaison between factory needs and Wahl Canada's needs. Usually, these meetings would consist of Scott, me, the US agent, the factory owner (Mr. Kung) and several assistants. The assistants were invariably female, and while they were not all the same, they usually had similar characteristics. They didn't usually speak until spoken to, they were very pleasant and very helpful. Their role was to take notes during the meeting, and if we wanted to see a product or a product alteration, they would run off and remarkably quickly come back with what we wanted to see. We might say, for example, I would like to see that in blue rather than red and even though they didn't make it in blue, they would be back so quickly, you would think they did.

One particular day, we were in one of these meetings. I had to answer the call of nature, and these meetings never seemed to stop other than for meals, so you just got up and went when you needed to. I went to their washroom, which was adjacent to the meeting room. It was not very big, but big enough for the job I needed to do. The walls were glass, similar to the bottom of old Coke bottles – very thick but opaque so nobody could see through. Without getting too graphic, let's just say I was tending to my business when a couple of fairly hearty noises went off. (Asian food can cause some adjustments to your system). I finished up and went back to the meeting. Scott leaned over to me and whispers in my ear "Did you fart in there?". Somewhat embarrassed, I whispered, "Yeah, why, did you hear it?". He says, "hear it? The whole fkn room shook!!". So imagine, while I thought I was off in privacy, the factory owner, the US agent, and all those female assistants heard this unmistakable rumbling. I had no idea!!! It is funny though, there may have been times through the years when people saw that Scott and I were in a meeting and while there was a chance the President and Vice President of Wahl Canada were discussing some high strategy, there is an equal chance that behind closed doors we were laughing like hell about the time I nearly blew up a showroom. He said that everyone in the room heard me very loud and clear.

You can imagine, the next year going back to that meeting, I sure heard from Scott a number of times jokingly "Don't you dare go to the can during our meeting!!!". We did go back, and sure as hell, midway through the morning, I had to go again! You can't make this stuff up! I did all I physically could to ensure that it was as quiet as possible, and I was pleased at the end when I had successfully completed the task at hand without blowing anything up. What could possibly go wrong? Well.......there was the issue of the flush. And sure enough, the toilet clogged!! I could not believe it. To further complicate things, there was no plunger in the bathroom. There was nothing I could do. I am pretty sure I started sweating. How do I go back in the meeting and tell everyone to stay away from the can because I plugged it up. Well, the first thing I had to do was tell Scott. I knew he was going to firstly, think I was pulling his leg, but once he realized I was serious, we might actually lose him for the rest of the day because he would be laughing so hard. I got back and whispered to him, "I clogged it, and there is no plunger". His first reaction was "You're joking?!". When I convinced him I wasn't joking, we both were on the verge of losing it. Now remember, we are in a serious business meeting, and if we both lose it, it is so disrespectful to the people we were meeting with so we did our best to hold it together. I was concerned that somebody else would need to go in there and they would be ambushed, so I had to do something. Mid-meeting, I walked over to the other side of the table and whispered in Mr. Kung's ear, "The toilet is clogged". He looked at me and said "what??" as if he didn't quite understand – his English is not the best. I repeated it, and he seemed to understand. He whispered into one of the assistant's ears, and she ran out of the room. A few minutes later, the door opens and along comes Mr. Fung, who is about 75 years old, and he shuffles around very slowly in slippers that look about 40 years old. Alongside Mr. Fung is one of those mop and buckets on wheels. It was very hard to pay attention to our meeting with Scott, and I trying not to laugh too hard. We watch as Mr. Fung goes into the bathroom. He comes out about 5 minutes later, shuffles slowly across the room and goes out the door. After about 5 minutes, here comes Mr. Fung again. He shuffles over to the bathroom and hangs on the door, a handwritten sign that says "OUT OF ORDER". At that point, you could have knocked Scott and me over with a feather, we were trying (and not succeeding) not to laugh so hard. I can't really tell you if we were able to get any business done that day, but I can tell you we sure laughed a lot!

I think I have summed up the highlights of my Asian travel. It was an experience I would never trade. I learned so much about people, travelling cultures, internationally, and I got to know some wonderful people in other countries. The friends I made in Taiwan, Singapore, China, Sri Lanka, the Philippines, and South Korea will be friends for life. I know I may not see them much now that I retired (or at all), but I know that if I were ever in their country, they would insist on taking me out for an evening of dinner and drinks, and I would always be looked after on my travels there. I consider myself extraordinarily lucky to have had that experience.

"I don't want you out there spending my money like a drunken sailor"

Building a good organization seems easy from the outside – hire good people, let them do their jobs and live happily ever after, right? In theory, that sure seems to be a good plan. In reality, it is one of the hardest things to do, and it starts with hiring people. I have seen so many organizations get held back from success by simply putting the wrong people in charge. But how is it that well- intentioned people who the majority of the time want the best for the company, end up hiring dolts?

I think there are several reasons that I have seen:

Hiring managers do not understand what the true needs of the job are. Too often, a resume gets someone "half-hired" before they walk through the door for their first interview. I have seen hiring managers talking excitedly about candidates before they have even walked through the door. "He has an MBA and has two years with Procter and Gamble and two more with Nestle – he looks great for the job!" Ugh....most times when a hiring decision turns out to be the wrong one, it is not because someone doesn't have the skills or the education – it usually turns out to be related to the type of person that is, and the fit with the environment. I worked at one company that had an International Sales Manager with an impeccable resume, but he was one of the most disrespectful people I've met in 43 years. However, because he looked good on paper, and the International business was young, and it was easy to achieve results, he managed to hold that position for nearly a decade. What the company missed was how much larger that division could have been (5-10x in my view) if they had just put the right person at the helm. The company did not do their job by monitoring staff sentiment and therefore this guy was able to do his thing for many years, costing the company tens of millions of dollars in untapped opportunities. It is so simple to determine how a leader is doing by just talking to a few key people who know him well, whether they are colleagues or subordinates. Their praise or criticism will almost always be related to how that person treats others (She is great, she has helped me so much) or the usual first phrase "he is an asshole" followed by "you should see the way he talks to people" or "he never responds to anything". These are the things hiring managers should be endeavouring to find out during interviews.

Hiring managers are hiring for the company's "audience" and not for the actual job itself. This is related to the above point, but a bit different. Often, managers are not secure in how they feel others view them, so they take the safe route and hire someone whose resume is bulletproof from criticism. After things go south, they have a built-in defence – "I am surprised it didn't work out, with that resume, I never could have seen that disaster coming". I remember at one company, an insecure manager hired a guy because "he has great experience from Procter and Gamble". Two months in, we were moving our offices, while the rest of us worked our butts off moving things in and out, this dude sat in his office reading magazines. You can't make that stuff up! And yes, I heard all the "well, he had great experience, we didn't know he was going to be like that". Don't get me wrong, nobody can predict with 100% accuracy what someone is going to be like, but there are certain things people can do to flesh out people's personalities and tendencies during interviews. I have found that an effective technique is to have candidates walk me through their career from start to finish. (and even before their business career starts) It enables me to ask questions like "when you made that decision, what were you thinking, why did you do that," and questions like that to get

And that is the simplest way to get beyond the resume – get the candidate talking about their life, not just their work, but their life. This gets you (if you are watching closely) insights into who they really are. It helps you figure out the important parts of a person – how they are likely to treat others, what they are going to be like to work with, what things do they like to discuss, and are they a positive, optimistic type or more of a Debbie Downer.

In addition to the above, I think it is very important to set a casual tone for the candidate – make them feel they can say anything to you. The more comfortable they are with you, the more they will share with you, and the better you will see who they truly are. And that is what is the most important part if you really want to boil it down to one single factor – you want to know who they "truly are". The more you find out who they "truly are," the more you will have an accurate view of whom you might be hiring, and therefore, you can visualize how they might get along with your key people.

There are times when even the best of intentions can go astray. I remember early in my career at Wahl, Scott had this feeling that our warehouse group was a bit too relaxed, and he wanted a bit of a whip cracked. We interviewed a bunch of people and found ourselves leaning towards a very qualified lady who had a bit of an edge to her. We hired her, looking forward to that bit of an edge, helping to make that group a little less relaxed. Well, suffice it to say, it did not work out well. Everything we did in the hiring process we did correctly. What we did not anticipate was the extreme extent of this "edge" that this lady carried with her. Within a couple of weeks, both Scott and I had people beating a path almost daily to our offices, and yes, there were tears! On the morning we decided to cut our losses and fire her, we left a voice message for one of her key people to meet us before work so we could discuss strategies for after we terminated her. Little did we know, this lady was actually checking her employees' voice messages, so that nearly blew up in our faces as she did her best to determine what was going on in this early morning meeting that she was not invited to. So we did hire someone with an edge, but nobody told us the edge was the edge of a guillotine – all we wanted was maybe the edge of a razor!!

There is also a strategy for being interviewed as well.   When I applied to work at Swenson Canada (which eventually became Wahl Canada), I had two interviews with Scott Fraser and Jack Swenson. These interviews went exceedingly well – in my mind, these were down-to-earth guys who were driven to succeed, and the little things didn't matter – it was all about results. At that time in my career, having become sick   of   the   big   corporate environments and the politics that went with them, this was a breath of fresh air for me. I simply wanted a job I could succeed at without a lot of the other BS. This was it – the needs were simple, as expressed by Scott. "We have a great brand that does very well in the Professional trade, and we think it will do well with consumers, but we currently do not have much distribution. If you think you can break down retailer doors, expand our distribution, and build our business, that is all we are going to be interested in. I don't care what time you come in, or how often, I just care that you can build the business". For me, this was perfect. I had had several jobs by then, and it became clear to me that selling was where I was best. I can talk to people, and people tend to trust me almost right away.

After two interviews, we were all set – one last obligation for me – "we need you to take this personality/aptitude test – it will help us understand how you like to be managed, who you are, and what type of environment you need to be the most successful". I took the test. Keep in mind, I knew full well what my weaknesses were, and I was pretty sure this test would expose me. My lack of patience for detail, my "don't really care about the numbers as long as I am doing the right things" approach, and my unrelenting devotion to the long-term, even at the cost of the short-term, were all open to exposure. I would like to tell you that I did the test with no hesitation. That would be a lie. I knew that I was risking a job I wanted very much by taking this test. I considered trying to "fool the test" by hiding some of the obvious weaknesses I had – this is usually pretty easy to do by just giving "middle of the road" answers and avoiding extremes. The problem was, I did, and still do, have extremely strong beliefs about a lot of things – not all of which are best for the corporate world. I ended up deciding that I was going to give them everything as honestly as I could and if it ended up costing me the job, it was probably doing me a favour because if "me being me" was not something they would like on a test, they sure as hell were not going to like working with me! That is one thing I have always encouraged people being interviewed – don't try to hide who you are – you might just do that, but all it is going to do is get you a job working with people who just might not like who you really are. So I did the test, and did it very honestly.

It was not long before I got the call from Scott – "Can you come in sometime soon, we want to discuss the test results with you?". This was a bit different from "do the test, and then we will put the offer together". I knew it....the real Frank was scaring them off. Scott started by saying that there were a number of good things on the test, but there were a couple of things that concerned them. He said, "Your attention to detail comes out 1 out of 100. This position is dealing with the biggest of the biggest retailers in the country – Walmart, Sears, Canadian Tire etc. I am very concerned about hiring you to deal with them when it looks like you have trouble managing the smallest of details." The key to this discussion was that Scott ended by saying "what do you think about this?". I have seen many managers in my career, and I mean many, that would not have had any more conversations with me – they simply would have said "we hired another candidate" and that would be it for me. This one result of mine alone would have scared them off of me. Not Scott – he wanted to hear what I had to say, and I am forever grateful for that approach and always used the same approach when I was hiring people.

Now....you want to know my response? Are you thinking like "how the hell did you talk yourself out of that one?". Well, Scott and I through the years many times looked at each other and said 'why don't we try honesty". So I did! I started out by acknowledging the result. "Yes, I understand the test shows that my detail orientation is weak and I 1000 percent agree with that reading on me. I do want you to know that I knew this very early in my career and have had to work to overcome it my entire career. There are people who can naturally organize things very quickly and maybe come up with a beautiful excel spreadsheet in 20 minutes. I can also come up with a beautiful excel spreadsheet but because of my lack of detail orientation, it might take me 5 times the effort it takes someone else. I do however work very fast so it has never been a problem in my jobs, as you can see, I have held some very responsible positions and have a track record of success so if this aspect of my personality had been a huge issue, I don't think I would have been able to achieve the results I have achieved so far in my career." The point is, as a hiring manager, too many are interested in the "AHA....gotcha" rather than identifying what the weakness is, and determining if it is something that is an insurmountable obstacle or something that can be worked with. Scott liked me, and therefore wanted to hear what my thoughts were on it. The main thrust of my answer was that I know I am very weak, therefore I work my butt off to compensate, and it seems to be working. Whew...made it past that one!!!!

Well...as I sat there all proud of myself for that one, he hit me with the next one. My risk-taking was 99% out of 100. Now, remember, this was before the company was owned by Wahl Clipper, so the money was 50/50 owned by Scott and Jack. Scott's quote I remember from 25 years ago was "I don't want you out there spending my money like a drunken sailor". I again answered honestly " I agree, my fear of risk is minimal, this comes from my inner belief that long term importance trumps short term importance every time so I don't mind taking risks if I have a good basis of evidence to support that it will be the right move in the long term.

Also, remember, just because I don't mind risk, that does not mean that I would take risks or do anything without the appropriate support from my Manager. I have always worked well and closely with my Managers, and I would anticipate the same with you. And by the way, you are interviewing someone who for the last 5 years was in his own business, so I think that already made it clear, risk doesn't bother me". Suffice it to say, Scott again was open to hearing my point of view, and he hired me, and we had one of the truly great business runs one could imagine together. People often thought of us as two peas in a pod or brothers from another mother. I think we only had maybe 3 serious disagreements despite working closely together for 25

~~Years~~was the most enlightened Manager I had the experience of working with.

Hiring is an art, not a science, and we would all do better to remember that. Despite all of the above, I have made some brutal hires through the years, but I have also made some of the greatest hires that to this day I am so proud of.

If I had to find one characteristic in common with some of my best hires, I would call it the down-to-earth scale. If they come across as "down to earth", that has almost always led to great hires. I can think of half a dozen or so who I had a feeling in the first 60 seconds that I wanted to hire, and that feeling was never wrong. On my list of great hires through the year, most of you know who you are, but in every case, there was something screaming at me in the first minute, "you are going to love working with this person!!". Karim, Pam, Sasan, Singying, Ryan, Rich, and Maureen – you were all "who I thought you were" and made me proud every day! It was the simple, unembarrassed "this is me" approach that got you the job, and because you were true to who you presented, it allowed you to succeed all these years. Again, if you had been misled in some way to "sell yourself into the job", all that would have resulted in is not a good fit between you and me, and probably would not have worked out so well.

"Nobody bats a thousand" ...

There were a couple of big lessons learned in my career, and I can think of two of them. Firstly, to understand the background, you have to remember, I continuously had this voice for most of my career telling me that I was not as good as many of the people I was dealing with. This traces right back to my lack of detail orientation – I just was not as on top of things as I perceived most people either were, or expected me to be. It encourages this feeling inside that I need to cover up my weaknesses because if people really knew how inept I was, they would never put their trust in me. In hindsight, it seems kind of silly when I look back and see all that I accomplished over 43 years, but throughout almost the entirely of my career, it was very real.

When I was in the business before Wahl, Retail Solutions, it was a small business with just myself and my partner. This was the ultimate in pretense – we were trying to sell American products into Canadian Retailers. We were the link and we had to create a credible impression with both sides so that they could trust us in making decisions on their behalf for hundreds of thousands if not millions of dollars at a time. I mean honestly, if they knew that it was just my partner and me, and that we played golf 3-4 times a week while running our business do you think they would really trust us? In our minds, we knew the answer to that. Don't get me wrong, we did work hard, usually early mornings, or later in the day or evenings, but during the day, we wanted to be golfing as much as we could. After all, our membership was paid, so we had to get our money's worth!! If they also knew that our company consisted of an office in my house in Aurora, and an office in my partner's house in Burlington, our credibility as a trustworthy Canadian company would take another hit. Remember, this was long before "work at home" was the commonplace it is today so having a standalone office was a badge of success. My badge of success frequently had dirty dishes and/or laundry hanging around – hardly conducive to establishing credibility with either the big American companies or Canadian retailers. I used to laugh to myself when I sold something to Walmart – "if only they knew what my office looked like". That was my little secret ☺

We had a time when we thought the big ship had come in for us. Through some of our American friends, we were introduced to the Founder of a Medical device called Doser. I don't recall the founder's last name, but I recall his first name was Jim, and this device was created out of a real-life need seen by Jim. Jim was at his nephew's soccer game one day, and his nephew had an asthma attack. Somebody ran and got his puffer, but when they went to use it on the child, the puffer was empty. As a result, the nephew had to be rushed to the hospital where This thankfully, he was saved.

could have cost him his life, though! Jim decided to do something about it, and he designed a product called Doser. It was a simple device that was to be attached to a puffer, and it simply counted the number of times the puffer was used. For example, if a puffer usually held 50 puffs, this would alert you that you were getting low before it ran out. Up to that point, the only way to know was to float your puffer in water, and that would somehow indicate you were getting low, but it was not exact. My partner and I loved this idea and took it to Shoppers Drug Mart. We had meetings with the highest of the high at Shoppers, and they were also very excited about this. We had the store people, the pharmacy people and everyone behind the scenes really excited about this launch. We allowed Shoppers to be the first retailer in the country to launch this item, so it enabled them to get the jump on their competition. Not only that, this was a product that would truly make a difference and could actually save lives. We worked with Shoppers to develop brochures for the pharmacists and patients, and could not wait until the launch! This was going to be the biggest product we had ever had. It turned out that we were slightly off in our thoughts. It was the biggest product we ever had if I add the word flop in right after product. How could we possibly screw that up? We had a great product invented for the right reasons, we had a very credible organization that agreed with us that this was great...what did we miss? What we all missed was asking consumers if they wanted to pay $50 for this little LED device to stick on the end of their puffer. They did not. I don't know if it was the cost or the hassle of dealing with another device on top of the puffer, but for whatever reason, Doser did not sell, and our job went from "counting the money" to trying to help Shoppers Drug Mart deal with all the inventory they had. Lesson learned – despite all the good signs around, companies might want to ask the consumer before they assume all is good.

You might think I learned that lesson very well since it was such a big part of my life. You would be wrong. There was another time at Wahl where we launched a beard trimmer, and it had a new feature – a vacuum! The selling angle was that women are going to love this because it will stop men from leaving a messy sink. Scott and I were very excited about this launch as we were at that point, a very weak #3 in the trimmer business in Canada. Again, we had a retailer very excited about it, and we launched with an early exclusive time period for Canadian Tire – they were the first retailer to bring it to Canada. They jumped all over it with advertising, displays, and lots of excitement. Lo and behold, we had another Flop with a capital F! Can you guess what happened? In the US, they were relatively successful with a $49 retail. In Canada, because of the exchange rate and a couple of other factors, we had to launch at

$79. This was like my Doser nightmare #2. The exact same issue as Doser – Great product, at a price too high for consumers to be interested. Yes, I do have a thick head sometimes!! The interesting part of this was that shortly after it was clear that this was not selling anywhere near what our expectations were, Canadian Tire changed buyers. We were quite happy with this change because we were living in dread of Canadian Tire coming back to us saying, "this stuff is not selling, take it all back". We had thousands of units out there and to buy them back would have been crippling for us. Eventually, we had to face the music. Our new buyer, Milton Tjin wanted to meet with us to review our products. In preparation for the meeting, we had all kinds of possible ways to deal with this problem. We must have gone over about 15 different scenarios of "how to handle" when the issue arose. Through the first half of the meeting, we discussed a lot of good things we were doing, and Milton was proving himself to be someone we could work very well with and partner with to grow our mutual business. He then came to the vacuum trimmer, and Scott and I sat silent as he viewed the numbers. He asked about the background and how we got to where we are, and after a short pause, he said words I will never forget: "Oh well...nobody bats a thousand....what's next?" I wanted to kiss him!! (If you are reading this, Milton, not really, that is just an expression☺)

There was a real learning there for us. We went in thinking he was going to be single-focused on the one thing we did wrong as a company – we had a product launch that didn't go well. Milton's mindset was that Wahl is a good company, who have done a lot of good things together with Canadian Tire, and is supportive of CTC, and they had one less than successful product launch. No big deal, let's find the next WIN for both companies. Our incorrect mindset came again from the inner voice telling us that we are not "the big boys," we are just Wahl. If I learned one thing in 25 years at Wahl, in hindsight, it is that customers value a good, reliable partner and know that no company is perfect.

My big secret...many years ago I won the lottery

 For anyone doubting that chapter title, it is absolutely true!! Let me use my own roundabout way of telling the story.

There are a lot of things that bother me nowadays about my life, and a lot of things that worry me.

To name a few:

Being recently retired, of course, I worry about money.

Being older now, of course, I worry about health.

Without getting too specific, politicians and their hypocrisies, corruption, and stupidity bother me a lot.

I loathe the way a trusted and supportive ally can be treated despite the fact that we have stood by our friends through times when maybe it wasn't so easy to stand up for them, but we did, and always will. Threats, ridicule, and tantrums are not the way to deal with a close relationship - talking and working together are. (This is being written in 2025, right in the midst of Donald Trump turning Canada into Public Enemy #1)

I worry about the health of people who matter to me - the older I get, the larger a concern this becomes.

I worry that I will never figure out a consistent golf swing. (Okay, I put that one in just for fun)

I am sure there are many other things that I could list that bother me, but I think you get the point.

Think about this.....Religious beliefs aside, man has been walking the earth for somewhere between 4 and 7 million years. Let's say I am fortunate enough to live to 80 years old. Those 80 years are approximately 1/100th of a percent of the time that man has existed. So in the scheme of things, that means there have been something like 87,500 blocks of 80 years during which I could have lived. Some of those included the worst periods in mankind's (Sorry Justin, it's mankind - NOT peoplekind!) history - there were eras where volcanoes darkened the earth, eras where plagues killed millions, war periods, and any number of atrocious periods of mankind. I was lucky enough to be born in this era. An era with lots of the above aggravations - but I would still choose this era over any other in history! Now, maybe someone in the future would look back on our era and say "Man, we are so much luckier than they were" but I am not in a position to talk from a future perspective - all I know is that right now, I feel very lucky to have been born during this time period. Think of all the bad things we don't have, but also think of all the good things we do have. Our ability to continue making our lives better through our ingenuity makes us all very lucky.

I was born in North America and have lived my entire life here. Think of all the places that I could have been born in. I could have been born into a famine region, one of the many regions where persecution for no reason takes place, a region hit particularly hard by poverty, violence or any other problematic region. But.....I wasn't. I have lived my life on the greatest continent in the world North America (subjective opinion) is 7.5% of) the world's population. Again, I beat the odds by ending up here.

Think about it. The odds I had to beat to not only be born in North America, but also be born in this period of time are pretty astronomical. On top of that, what are the odds of someone being born today into a great family and being surrounded by great people their entire life? We all have had enough discussions about family and personal problems to know that one is far from guaranteed to be born into a great family, even if they are born in the right time period on the right continent. Now add to that the odds of being very healthy, and I truly have beaten a lot of odds to get to where I am today. We all know a lot of people who are not nearly as lucky.

Now...back to the chapter title. I think you know it already, but yes, many years ago, when I was born, I "won the lottery" by being born in North America, during this time period, to the family I was born into and to be as healthy as I am. The purpose of writing this is to say that I know many people who also won the lottery because they have a lot of those factors in common with me and my circumstances, but you wouldn't know it from talking to them. I must admit, I forget how lucky I am often, but every time I think about it, it changes my attitude because if just one of those variables above had turned out differently, I would be in a far less fortunate position than I am. I would also suggest that many of you also won the lottery, and I hope this little reminder might add something to your day.

The better you are, the less you have to say

Obviously, in 43 years I have seen a lot of people and how they try to manage their relationships and their careers. The single most misunderstood principle is "how to get noticed". People think that dominating conversations, making sure their point of view is heard, volunteering for high-profile assignments, and any number of other chances to jump into the spotlight is the way to maximize exposure for your skills and your career. I could not say this any more clearly – WRONG, WRONG, AND WRONG. If you doubt that even for a second, go back and look at it. I capitalized every word so that there could be no misinterpretation – it is wrong. As the chapter title says, the better you are, the less you have to say.

You might want to challenge that – you can go into meetings and say nothing and come out, and nobody knows how good you are because you said nothing. Fair point...on the surface, you are correct. Like most things in my career, I view things like this through a longer-term lens than just one meeting. If there is a particular meeting where maybe there is a discussion about a point of interest that is your expertise, and you think you can help get things to a solution, by all means, do not keep quiet – speak up.

My point is that as a general rule, in the longer term, people will get to know you. Whether you are an unabashed braggart, or a Wall

Flower, over time, people will get to know you and how good you are. You can oversell by being an unabashed braggart and people will find out in time that you really are not as good as you say you are. You can also be very shy, and not say too much, or undersell your skills, but over time, people will get to know how good you are.

This is where I think my philosophy helps in career management. If you accept that regardless of how you choose to approach letting people know about your skills, that they are going to know the true picture over time, then the simple question becomes – what kind of person do I want to be? Do I want to be someone who is always out front telling others how good they are? From my experience, you don't want to be "that guy". It comes across to others as conceited, know it all, and aggressive. Conversely, should you choose to be less aggressive about how good you are, others will see that humility and it will become part of how you are viewed by others.

The Best time to show people they matter....

As a manager, we often think that when we have a good interaction with people, this helps them to understand that they matter to us. I have found there are times in relationships when we have profound opportunities to show people they matter. Those times are simple enough – when people need us, we have the greatest opportunity to show people they matter.

A few years ago at Wahl, we had a husband and wife team working there – the husband worked in the warehouse, and his wife worked up front Administration. (Finance, Order Desk). They were a young couple, young children, house with a mortgage etc. They came to us one day and said that they had some health issues. In short, she needed a kidney transplant and he was a match for her. What this meant to the company was that they would both be off work for an extended period – maybe 6 months or so. Scott and I were both involved in the "how do we handle this" part for the company. I remember this to be one of the shortest conversations we ever had – we both thought "these are good people, let's keep them whole throughout this process". In other words, we didn't want them to have financial worries, or job worries on top of everything else they were going through. We very quickly told them to do what they had to do, and the company would continue to pay them until they came back to work. It is an unusual gesture for a company to make as we have quite a generous government unemployment plan in Canada but it would not have replaced their salary. Admittedly, larger companies cannot do this because there are written policies that companies have to follow. We were not so constrained at that point as we were still a small company (albeit growing very quickly) and did not have black and white policies in this area yet. It was one of the things I loved about being with the company at that time – we were small enough that we could really make a difference in people's lives through actions like this. They were tremendously grateful and long story short, the operations were successful and both came back to work. This is one of those times where it didn't quite work out the way we had intended. In her first week back after six months or so off, the wife informed us she had accepted another job. Needless to say, we were furious. We had supported her for six months when we didn't have to and she came back and quit on us. It was one of the worst betrayals of the employee-employer relationship I saw in my 43 years but it happens. If she had waited a few months and then done it, it would not have been a big deal. The fact that it was the first week tells me she was accepting our salary while planning to leave us. If I were in the same circumstances again, I would not change a single part of our actions. I think the vast majority of people would have appreciated the over and above efforts we made on their behalf.

We had an employee at Wahl who had eye trouble. He worked in our warehouse, and he had some kind of degenerative eye disease. His vision deteriorated over the last ten years I worked at Wahl. At first, it got to the point where he could no longer drive a forklift – a major part of his job. No problem we decided – we will just find other work for him to do so that we can keep a good employee. It got to the point where he had to take an extended period off (months not years) to have surgery. This was a guy that did not have a lot of savings and was a live day to day kind of a guy. We again decided to pay him while he was off. We did it because it was the right thing to do for a good employee, but we had no idea the side benefit it would create for us. This guy was so vocal in the ensuing years, raving about how good the company was to him during his time of need. Those kinds of things were what made my job really enjoyable – I loved being in a position where I could really help people when they needed it.

Years ago we hired a National Account Manager. He was barely with us more than a few months when he got word that his Dad was sick and he was needed overseas. We told him at the time to "do what he needed to do for his family' and we would be here for him however we could. This was really a no-brainer decision. I loved that he was that close with his family and felt that kind of responsibility to his parents and his family. I hope when my time comes, that my kids will take on the kind of responsibility that he did.   It ended up a bit of a protracted journey to his Father's passing but he was able to be there for whatever he was needed for. He has since mentioned our actions to me many times and how much he appreciated the support of the company. It would not be a stretch to think that he has probably talked about it with his family, his friends and other people in our industry. Again, let me reiterate, that is not the reason we did stuff like this.   In all the above examples, we took those actions because it was the "right thing to do" – everything else is just the side story of the actions.

I remember many times with different Managers where I was

treated differently when sales were not what Management thought they were. I used to say "one month I am a hero, and the next month I am a complete idiot." I understand the pressure Managers feel to keep the numbers coming but on the other hand, it makes you feel like you are only valued during the good times. I always tried to support good employees through the bad times because I felt that was a major opportunity to show a good employee how much I valued them. There is nothing more impactful then when an employee has had a tough month, where maybe a number of things have gone wrong for them and they are down on themselves to have a Manager say to them "Don't worry about it, keep doing what you are doing and things will turn around – you are still My Guy". That bit of support during tough times is worth its weight in gold to people. It is similar to the Canadian Tire example I used a few chapters back when our buyer said "nobody bats a thousand". It shows that what is important to you as a Manager is the person and what that person can do for you. Longer term, this will help ensure that you do get the best out of that person. It is a pretty simple concept – it is easy to be nice when times are good – that is not hard at all. It is much tougher to be nice during the pressure-filled tough times, but that is the time when it can have a long-lasting impact on people in terms of telling them where they really stand with you.

In every example above, there were people who needed help and we were there for them because it was "the right thing to do". The obvious benefit is to the individuals we helped.   Think about all the other benefits though:

☐Employee's friends and family hear about what a great company the employee is working for. This makes the employee feel good as well.
☐A good name amongst industry colleagues can influence future prospective employees.
☐Trust increases amongst the people involved leading to a better working relationship. The people above who stayed with Wahl were great supporters due in part to the

actions we took when times were tough.

To close this chapter out, the key point is, the best time to show people they matter is when they need you the most. That's when the true leaders show up and the "for show" leaders show who they really are.

"You can't go 200 miles an hour and all of the sudden stop"

In late 2018, I was speaking with a friend of mine who was retired. At this time, I was at the height of my "busyness" with Wahl. I was President of Wahl Canada (my full time gig ☺), and I had a side-hustle with Wahl, which was my position as Manager of 23 countries in Asia. As I detailed in the Asia chapter, this was a pretty significant side-hustle – I had to put more effort and time into my Asian duties than I did for my Canadian responsibilities. In short, I had an awful lot on my plate. Knowing I was getting close to 60, my friend said to me, "You better start looking ahead to retirement, you need to stop doing Asia well before you retire so that you can ease into retirement. You can't go 200 miles an hour, and just stop when retirement comes. You need to slow it down to maybe 100 miles an hour so that the transition to retirement is not such a shock to your system when it hits". I considered that very good advice, so in early 2019, I mentioned to Scott that at the end of 2019 (I turned 60 in November of that year), I would like to give up my Asian responsibilities and "just" be President of Wahl Canada. As usual with Scott, he was extremely supportive and fully understood why I wanted to do that. He was able to make that happen for me – just one of many things I am eternally grateful to him for. My second last trip to Asia was in November of 2019. I returned from that trip and made an off-hand comment to my wife that "something was happening in China. I heard lots of talk on that trip about a quickly spreading disease in China. It had not yet hit the media, but people who lived there and did business there were talking pretty openly about how many people were getting sick with this disease. I had one more trip to Asia in January of 2020 to

hand over my responsibilities, but I avoided going to China.
(Philippines, Taiwan and Korea).
As you probably know by now, the timing for me ending my trips to Asia turned out to be fantastic.

I woke up on the morning of March 12, and started my day as usual by checking my phone for emails/messages. I had a text from my daughter telling me that the NBA had just announced that their season would be cancelled immediately. Thus began one of the most extraordinary times in my 43 career.

In very short order, all of our lives would be facing major changes and my work-life took turns I never could have predicted or managed. It tested every aspect of our ability to manage our business. I was in a very unique position as I was responsible to the Wahl family for managing their business properly through that challenging time, while at the same time making sure that we as a company did everything right for our 40+ employees, and our customer base. I never could have imagined the number of tests that I would face over the next couple of years.

On March 11, my world was fine. Less than two weeks later, myself and my Management group were truly thrown into the deep end of the pool and told to swim. On March 23, our Premier of Ontario, Doug Ford, ordered all non-essential businesses to close. That was test number one – what do we do? The first thing we did was try to determine where we fell in the realm of essential versus non-essential. By the letter of the law, we were deemed essential as we fell into the personal grooming category and personal grooming was deemed to be an essential service. We knew were on legally safe ground by declaring ourselves essential and staying open. On the flip side, we had a workforce that was rightfully scared of coming to work. There was near hysteria about anything that added additional human contact to people. It did not feel right to me to face our employees and tell them it was essential that Canadians have access to hair clippers during this pandemic. If I had been an employee, I would have viewed that as a company simply using the letter of the law to stay open and make money. What's the worst thing that can happen if people don't have access to a hair clipper – hair grows!! Our first big decision was to close the company for two weeks in accordance with the Provincial order for non-essential businesses because it was "the right thing to do". It clearly was not a good thing for our business. In fact, the shutdown could not have come at a worse time for us. Our biggest business was selling hair clippers and that was one of the most affected businesses from the pandemic. Demand for hair clippers rose by at least a 5x factor overnight! Barber shops were one of the key industries closed down so people felt they would have no way of cutting their hair if they did not buy a hair clipper – that is why our business went through the roof overnight. If not for the pandemic, my first reaction would be that this is like a dream come true. After 20 years of selling hair clippers, I had learned that while hair clippers is a good solid business, it was never a high profile category. We were not Campbells soup, Heinz Ketchup, or Kellogg's or any of the super high volume products that were really important to our retail customers. We were a nice category but really an under the radar category. Overnight, we became more important that just about any category other than toilet paper. Retailers who I had been chasing for years to buy hair clippers, were all of a sudden on the phone trying to get us to sell them our product. It was like we were the cool kid at the dance, if not for the reason behind it, it truly would have been fun (I thought!) . I have never seen anything like the demand for our product. I remember one conversation with London Drugs, a drug retailer in Western Canada, where they pretty much said, "Send us whatever you have, we will take it". This wasn't even Walmart, Costco or Canadian Tire, this was a regional retailer, so you can imagine the demand from the National Retailers. I do have to commend our base of Canadian retailers – despite the desperation to get product, every retailer respected the fact that we had shut down our operations for two weeks in order to give our employees a chance to digest all of this and keep them safe. Our employees also very much appreciated what we did because they understood how hard it was for us to do that at the very time when our customers needed us most. I will also commend the Wahl Headquarters in the US – they were extremely supportive of the approach we were taking.

I remember how surreal it was the 1-2 times I went into the office during the shutdown to see empty offices. It just feels really weird to go into your building when you know it is a business day and the lights are off and nobody is in their usual workplace. It really brings home that something serious is happening.

We reopened after the two-week closure, but even that was a hard decision. We had to open because there was so much pressure from customers for us to get back in business – they needed our product. We had everybody who could work from home stay at home but you cannot ship product from home so we had to have the warehouse staff back in. Needless to say, we bent over backwards with our safety precautions but we did still have a business to run.

The next problem we had to face was "who gets our product". That was really tough. While at first I thought it was great that our product was in such high demand, it was not very long before I realized how this rise in demand was really not a blessing, it was more of a curse. We had Walmart, Costco, Canadian Tire, and any number of regional retailers demanding our product, and we had nowhere near enough product to make anyone happy, so we literally had to pick who gets what.

We did our best to keep as many customers happy as we could, and we also tried to ensure that we didn't send too much to any one retailer because we would rather have product get sold right away than give a retailer the ability to have a month's inventory on the shelves.

This did lead me to one major disappointment. Many retailers have a "fine" policy in place for suppliers who cannot ship product. This is in place to ensure that if a company is terrible at supplying them, the supplier feels the pain so that they have an incentive to fix it in a hurry. A more cynical point of view might be that it is a way to ding suppliers for extra cash. Everyone knew the type of pressure that a sudden increase in demand places on a manufacturer, and the amount of extra demand pressure on us was unprecedented. There was no way, no matter how good we were as a company, that we could keep up with that kind of demand, so there were clearly going to be product shortages. On top of that supply chains for nearly all goods were very quickly overwhelmed leading to shortages in just about every product category. Nearly every retailer in the country that had a fine policy in place waived fines for the duration of the pandemic for us, as they understood the challenges we faced. There was one notable exception – Walmart. I argued and argued until I was blue in the face, yet Walmart hit us with fines like I had never seen before. I will not divulge the amount, but let's just say it was hugely significant. It bothered me very much (still does), that Walmart would take advantage of their strength in the marketplace to hit us with what I thought were very unfair fines. They punished us with fines, despite the fact that the shortages were pretty much outside of our control. Remember what I said earlier about supporting people during tough times – the lack of support from Walmart during our toughest times was something that was not easily forgotten. While we were able to get some discounts on the fines (Thank you Dianne!), the fact that we were fined at all while we were all going through an unprecedented pandemic should make every Walmart executive look at themselves in the mirror.

I have outlined above the pressure we went through from our customers. On the other side of things were our efforts to get product. Anyone familiar with manufacturing will understand how difficult it is to react to the ridiculous increases in demand we were going through. As a global corporation, it was not just Wahl Canada that was experiencing this, but every Wahl subsidiary worldwide was going through the same thing, so the demands placed on the Wahl supply chain were impossible to satisfy. In Canada, we had to make decisions about which customers would get product. Worldwide, Wahl had to make decisions about which countries would get product. There are so many factors to consider when making those decisions – most of it comes down to "who is going to play the biggest role in determining our success going forward when all of this settles down". As such, countries such as the USA were a focus for the organization. Walmart Canada may have been very important to my business in Canada, but our sales were nothing when compared to Walmart USA, Target, or Amazon USA. We had to (rightfully) fight tooth and nail within our own organization to get anything we could because every hair clipper they gave to Canada was one less that those big US retailers would receive. I must say, while at the time it was hard to recognize, that our company did a fantastic job of keeping as many people happy as we could.

Our safety procedures in the warehouse slowed down our productivity significantly. We had people off sick (covid or symptoms), we had more procedures to be followed, and we had an urgency to get stuff done quickly, driven by the customer's need to get product. It is a wonder we all didn't snap, but again, in hindsight, we came out of it as well as I think one could expect.

Like most things in the pandemic, seemingly good news was never that simple. I remember the relief I felt when the vaccines started to become more available. It was time to start getting everyone back in the office. I chose to trust that the vaccines overall were a good thing, as I really didn't know at the time, but if enough of the medical people were saying it was good, who was I to argue with them. I was more than thrilled when I heard that not only does taking the vaccine help you "not get" Covid, it also helps you to "not spread" the disease. We met to discuss this as a management group. The subject to discuss was how to handle the vaccines. Ultimately, we came down on the side of keeping everyone safe. I did not want someone to be in possible danger because they were sitting at their desk, and someone next to them was unvaccinated and therefore more able to spread the disease. We instituted a policy in conjunction with our "back to the office" plan, which said that everyone needed to be vaccinated in order to come back to the office. Out of 40 people, we had two who would not have gotten the vaccine if we had not issued that order. While I did feel bad for ordering someone to have something done that maybe they didn't believe in, I comforted myself in the fact that I had a duty to do all I could to protect people sitting at their desks who didn't want unvaccinated people sitting next to them. I had discussions with the two people (both of whom I respected very much) and told them that while I respected their right to feel the way they did, for the greater good, I had to stand my ground. They knew that if they did not get vaccinated, it would cost them their position. This was not something I took lightly, and I hated doing it, but again, I was thinking of the others who wanted their co-workers to be as safe as possible. I could not have lived with myself if I had had someone unvaccinated come to work, get someone else sick, who would then possibly have taken that home to their families. People could have died because I was too weak to enforce what was generally seen as the right policy for the time.

Hindsight is 20/20. Now, several years later, I regret that policy. I do not regret that we did it – based on the information we had at the time, I would do the same thing again. What I do regret is that the information we were being fed at the time was clearly wrong. We didn't know it at the time, but I think it is very clear now that two aspects of the medical expert's opinions were wrong – I believe that the vaccines did do some good, but I do not believe, based on all that I have seen, that it did anything to prevent spread nor stop you from getting the disease. There are just way too many stories of people who were vaccinated and still spread it, and of course, many who still got the disease. I believe that the vaccine probably did a very good job of lessening symptoms when you actually did get the disease. I do not believe the vaccine had much affect when it came to either catching or spreading the disease. I know there are probably medical people who will disagree but this is what I saw. As such, I really regret that two people who did not want to get vaccinated did end up getting vaccinated because of me. That is something I will have to live with and all I can do is say "sorry" to the two – and I have.

"Is one of you Colin Day?"

I remember in the very early days, as Wahl was becoming a global company, HQ decided to bring into HQ the worldwide Sales Managers. The thinking was, as it is with most meetings, that there would be a benefit to having everyone meet each other and spend time together.

Our Global HQ is located in Sterling, Illinois, USA – a small town of about 15,000 people right in the heart of the midwestern US. People there are down-to-earth, hard-working, religious, just a bunch of really good dudes and dudettes. Nearby, there is a town called Dixon, Illinois, whose claim to fame is that Ronald Reagan was born there. Dixon also has a population of about 15,000 people and is a 15-minute drive down the highway from Sterling.

On the first night before our meetings, the company organized a very nice dinner out in Dixon. We had a private room at a nice restaurant and a table that sat probably 30 people. I ended up sitting next to my counterpart from England – a very nice guy named Colin Day (Name changed to protect the innocent, or in this case, the guilty). We had a great time -for a group just getting to know each other, we seemed to be very lively and happy to be out on this very nice night. After dinner, the booze had flowed pretty generously, and the hair started to come down. One of the ladies was bragging about her falsies, and to prove to the cynics that she had them, she pulled them out and slapped them on the table. Colin, whose company I had enjoyed very much during dinner, apparently was not going to be outdone by a pair of falsies. He left for a while. When he returned, he was carrying a drink tray and prancing around like a waitress. He was pretending to be a very sexy waitress taking drink orders. He had commandeered one of the waitress's aprons so with the tray and the apron, he might have been able to pull it off except for one thing. The apron was one of those that went well down in the front but was open in the back. It wasn't long before we started to notice – this guy was bare-ass naked under that apron!!! There was lots of nervous laughter once that became apparent. I was unimpressed when he took his seat right next to me. That was about as bad as it got for the night, and that was that. We ended the evening and went back to our hotel. We were to show up at HQ at 8 am the next day so Colin and I went for breakfast about 7 at one of the many local restaurants. There were only two of us in the place and we were halfway through our breakfast when the waitress came over to us and asked 'Is one of you Colin Day?'. It turns out there was a phone call for him. We were shocked. How did anyone find us? After a brief call he came back to the table, and it looked like he had seen a ghost. When I asked what happened, he said that the call was from Mike Fliss (Global VP @Wahl and 2nd in command to Greg Wahl – in other words, a Big Wheel) and that he was not to go to the meeting this morning, he was to go to HQ and meet with Greg Wahl. It turns out they frown on nudity at corporate functions at Wahl – Who Knew??? They sent Colin home to the UK on the next flight. Needless to say, that was the topic of discussion during our meeting breaks. It seemed the locals were more offended than the rest of us. Most of us from other places had seen that type of behaviour or worse at sales meetings. In those days, sales meetings were still mostly a big drunk – that did change, but I would not say until the 2010s or so.

I felt sorry for Colin – I tried to imagine the call from Sterling to Colin's boss in the UK. "You are sending him home because he did what???" Or Colin's call to his family.....what do you say? I did feel for him – he was a fun guy to hang around with although had we become friends, I would have had to lay down the law – if we were to remain friends, the ass must remain covered! I think that is a reasonable request amongst friends.

We had one other episode that started in Dixon during my career there. Stephen Kay and I were in town for a meeting, and they took us out to Dixon for dinner. I was driving a rental car. We had a great dinner, and we were on the way back to our hotel in Sterling, just cruising up the highway after a good night. We were talking and laughing about the day's events and out of nowhere, I saw the flashing lights behind me. Shit!!!

I had forgotten all about watching my speed. I was fined for doing 91 miles per hour – I think the speed limit was 65 or so. The fine was over $200!! The funny thing about this was the next morning, in my meeting at HQ, it seemed every other person knew about it. Apparently they have some kind of crime report there, and I made the news!! Months later, I was at a restaurant and we were talking to the waitress, and she was telling me about this visitor to Wahl months back that was caught doing "nearly 100 mph"!! Sigh.....small towns!

Support versus honesty

As a Manager, my mind was constantly asking me the question, "Am I doing the right thing"? This pertained to many things, but in particular when it came to the employees who reported to me. I always tried to remind myself that my role was to assist however I could in helping them achieve success. If they were successful, there is every likelihood that I was also going to be successful. In my mind, that is probably the most important rule of leadership to remember – Be an Agent of Success. Even if you are not yet a manager, spend your time helping others become successful, and you will, before you know it, be thought of as a leader, and leadership roles will likely follow.

I want to dig a bit deeper, though. "Be an Agent of success" sounds like a pretty simple concept on the surface, but it is one of the most complex concepts I have come across in my career. If I accompany an employee of mine to an Interdepartmental meeting, maybe my idea of success is that two departments end up working together to solve a problem. Perhaps my employee's definition of success is a bit different. Perhaps my employee wants to successfully complete his or her presentation in the meeting and handle all subsequent questions as a means to reinforce to themselves that they are really learning and understanding the matters at hand. There is no hard and fast rule of how to handle these discrepancies but in the grey areas, I always went back to one of my bedrock rules – "when in doubt, talk about it."

I can think of a time when an employee of mine was doing a presentation, and a pattern started to emerge. Frequently, when he made an internal presentation, there were errors in spreadsheets. The spreadsheets were a small part of the presentation, and it was clear a ton of work had gone into the preparation. I am pretty sure that in his mind, as a new Account Manager, his goal for the meeting was to show the group that he had his customers under control and understood their business and how to maximize our business with them. He may well have done that, but the constant errors on the spreadsheet were of a major concern to me. I could have gone "big picture" with him and complimented him on all the really good work he put into the preparation, and that was certainly part of what I said. However, there was a pretty strong rebuke given because of the errors on the spreadsheet. Based on the way I usually am, (Big picture), you might wonder why I was so tied up on an error on a spreadsheet – haven't we all done that? We certainly have all done that, myself included. The reason this was such a big deal to me was that errors on a spreadsheet put his success both internally and externally at serious risk. He was responsible for a lot of dollars, and I knew from experience, if a customer found an error in a spreadsheet, he was not going to trust the information we were giving to him, so I wanted to make it clear – spreadsheets need to be Double and triple checked. The same would go for an internal meeting. He could be presenting to Senior Management who make decisions on his career, and a stupid little error on a spreadsheet can damage his credibility with people at higher levels who are usually prone to making snap judgments. So my seemingly "nit-picky" nature on this subject was actually borne out of a great desire to ensure he was as successful as he could possibly be. I am sure at times it seemed like I was being a prick but you have to do that sometimes.

Scott and I had many discussions about this kind of dilemma. We both started out as "nice guys" but before long we realized that being the nice guy meant sometimes being the taskmaster in the moment. In other words, I could be a really, nice guy and ignore the fact that the person sitting in front of me has a spot of ketchup running down his cheek just before he is about to meet the President of the Company. That is not being a nice guy – that is setting him up for failure. Being a nice guy is alerting him to the ketchup. That is a pretty graphic example that makes it easy to see why being a nice guy is just being honest. It is harder when it comes to business actions to see that being direct is actually being the nice guy.

I remember in my closing years at Wahl, we were going to receive a visit from Brian Wahl, our worldwide CEO. This is a big deal! I met with a couple of our Senior

Managers ahead of Brian's visit and one in particular from the Finance side of the company, had dug up what we did many years ago when we had a Senior Manager from Head Office visit, and he took the time to update the slides to today's business. As we were running through our dry run, it occurred to me that this was exactly that – a very dry run. It was boring as hell! There were lots of facts and figures, and our business was good, but even a good story can put you to sleep if not told properly. I was nearing retirement, so my mind was already on ensuring that my team looked good for Brian so that they would be okay going forward. I stopped the dry run and, as delicately as I could, which was not very delicate, I told them to scrap this presentation and start over. We discussed how to change it so that it was more in line with what Brian would be interested in. I am sure my message was not well-received at the time, but I am also sure that the new approach allowed them to be much more successful than they would have been. The secret to success for this presentation was really not a secret at all. If you are thinking about what someone might like to see in a results-oriented meeting, look at what they have been doing. In this case, I had the team look at some of the key programs that we all knew Brian was pushing at Head Office and how they might have affected us. An example would be that we spent significant time talking to Brian about each HQ Intitiatives (some of them newly created by Brian), how they are affecting us, what we like and don't like, and why. This turned out to be much better received than a bunch of numbers talking about past results.

There are other times though, where as a Manager, you might decide to let someone go ahead with something that you don't think is right because it is not a major problem. Letting people proceed in that scenario is giving them an opportunity to learn. Let them make the mistake themselves and often it will stick with them for a long time. Early on in my career, I misspelled a customer's name on a presentation, and I got hammered for it. You can bet – I never did that again!

I did not let this presentation to Brian go ahead in the "dry-number" format and have the people face the consequences because it can be bad for your career to have your presentation to the CEO turn out to be boring.

Promotions

Promotions are a subject that is discussed frequently in Management meetings. Discussions around promotions frequently draw out some pretty strong emotions.

As a Senior Manager, I viewed promotions in several ways. Firstly, they were a tool to help keep employees that we didn't want to lose. If you think back to an earlier chapter, the number one reason that employees leave organizations is that they do not feel respected. Promoting someone is a tremendous way to show that person that they are respected – it helps fill up that respect tank I talked about earlier. I always viewed my good employees as people worth exerting an effort to keep. Money was one way to do it. If an employee is paid well in his position compared to what other companies are going to pay for a similar role, then it makes it difficult for the employee to leave for a similar role. On rare occasion, an employee will get another job offer at a level of responsibility higher (promotion) than they are currently. In those cases, I was always comfortable losing someone because we clearly had decided we were not going to promote them at that point in time and if we had managed them correctly, we already would have told them a potential time frame that we were considering for promotion. So, if they know all of that and still decide to leave, good for them! I was almost always happy for the employee although I frequently missed them after they were gone.

A very common challenge of promotions in corporations is that there are more deserving people (and people who think they are deserving) then there are jobs to be promoted to. Most of the companies I worked for tended not to have high turnover and what this created was a high number of really good performers in their roles for long periods of time. This resulted in many employees saying to us, "I am doing a good job, why am I not being promoted?" We had several answers for that, and as usual, they focused on honesty. Sometimes the truth was that we were not an overly large company, and we were not management-heavy, so the harsh reality was that there were not a great number of jobs at the top. We would lay out the choice for the employee – stay where they are with a very good company that they can generally be happy with, or jump and take the chance that they find a company as good. If we were doing our job properly, we would have paid the employee well enough to make that jump difficult, and we had them at as high a position in the company as we saw fit for the near future. If, after all that, they did jump, then you shake their hand and congratulate them for taking a step forward in their career. Other things we did for those long-term employees in that position was at times, we would give them a new title. It did not change their day-to-day responsibilities, but it did give them a nice show of respect to help them feel appreciated.

One other aspect surrounding promotions was the actual work to be done. I had to ensure despite any employees' reaction or feelings, that I had the right person running a department because those people were going to be critical to our success as an organization. I remember one person came to me one day and said, "What do I need to know about decision-making when it comes time in the future for me to be seeking promotion". I remember putting together a whole list of subjects that will be considered at the time. Its funny because I have seen several people say something similar to this "I don't get it. I have come in, done this job, done it very well, and have succeeded beyond their expectations for x number of years (nowadays it's 2 years, when my career started it was 5 years!) and they still won't promote me". That is usually followed by a comment about what a cheap company they work for. The reality is that successfully doing a job is a very small part of what goes into deciding to promote someone.

Here is a list of some of the questions that are usually discussed when it comes time to consider promotions:

How are this person's interpersonal relationships? Do they get along with others? Are they respected by others, not just in the job they currently hold, but would they be respected as a leader?

How will Senior Management view this individual as a Manager? Will his or her appointment help to create the impression that we are competent in the way we are handling the business?

How will this person's peers react to their appointment as a Manager? I have seen cases where an announcement of a promotion was greeted with a standing ovation from the company. That is when you know you have really scored.

Some of the factors that will answer those questions the person making the decision will be, do others follow you? Do others come to you for your opinion? Can you be seen as a leader?

There are so many intangibles – I can understand the frustration of someone saying, "I did x, now they owe me y". The reality is that they do not owe you anything – the only obligation they have is to do what they think will work best for the business.

The casual remark

I heard a very casual remark 30 years ago that stuck with me until today and kept me from making similar mistakes many times in my career. I was with my partner at Retail Solutions, and we were negotiating an agreement with Shoppers Drug Mart. The gentleman at Shoppers Drug Mart said to my partner, "I would like you to fund some support for this product so we can promote it.". My partner, trying to get a deal done, answered "I am sure we can come up with one or two points (Percentage points) to help with that". The buyer immediately said, "I'll take 2," and therefore he gained two points to promote the product with. At the time, I remember laughing at my partner about how easily he got taken, but as someone who also likes to be conciliatory and try to make deals, I never forgot about how easily my partner threw away what probably amounted to about $20,000/year.

Don't fall in love with your title

~~When I was~~ with Neilson-Cadbury, my biggest customer was Loblaw Companies – a sister company of Neilson-Cadbury and Canada's largest grocery chain. I was young; this was my first job as an Account Manager, and the customer I had was a very important customer to our company.

Needless to say, when Loblaw said "Jump," I asked how high? There was a gentleman there who was a buyer. He was responsible for the wholesale business that Loblaws had, and it was a very big part of our business. This guy could have told me to walk through the office naked while swinging a rubber chicken, and my only question would have been "where do I get the chicken?". He knew that, and he knew he was very important to many of the companies that called on him to do business. He abused that position ridiculously. He was always looking for free samples from companies and money to support various charities. In the 2 years I dealt with him, I bet there was not a single week when he didn't demand something, and some of these demands were worth some serious value. He had companies delivering stuff to his home garage. I was too young to know anything about what was going on – the only thing I knew was that my sales numbers were doing well with him, so my job was secure. He was also not at all humble in how he did things. I saw him one day humiliate a young male staffer in front of me as the staffer was trying to help him figure something out, and he just ran up one side of this poor guy and down the other. Needless to say, in the community of suppliers who serviced him, the talk was of "what a jerk this guy could be, but he was very loyal to those of us who supported him," so we continued to do so.   Business increases drive a lot of decisions in the corporate world!

One day, out of the blue, I heard that he had been fired. I kept in touch with him longer than most, I would imagine.   Throughout my career, I always tried to be "that guy" who kept in touch when people were let go. I had heard early on in my career somebody say how surprising it was that the phone calls stopped the minute their jobs disappeared. How sad that seemed to me, and how superficial it seemed to make our relationships. I never felt relationships were superficial, so I never stopped reaching out to people who were going through tough times. In this case, though, this gentleman, after being fired, behaved as if he still was riding high in the corporate world. He soon found out from a lot of people that he thought were friends, that they were only compliant friends while he held the strength imbalance in the relationship. When he no longer had the big job, he found out just how quiet those phone lines could be. I felt sorry for him in a small way – I know he made his own bed, but he was not mentally equipped to figure out what had happened. He had submerged himself so deeply into his high-riding persona that he never realized that people were after his sales dollars and were not true friends. It was an early lesson for me to never forget that business is about relationships and not about the position one might hold at the time. I saw repeatedly that people who at one time held important positions became "just another guy" after exiting the big job. I am so glad I learned that lesson so early in my career.

The impact of leadership

One of the most misunderstood aspects of leadership is the impact we leaders have on others. Most of us really don't understand how much we headspace we can own in our employees' heads. Think about it – when we get together with other employees to talk shop how long is it before the subject of the Bosses comes up.

Being a leader, one has to realize that every action you take while seemingly simple on the surface can have a huge impact – this goes both ways – good and bad.

One of the times that drove this home the most graphically for me came when I was a few years into my employment at Wahl. I was convening a meeting of several people in the company to address an issue we were facing. I like to think of myself as someone good at bringing out people's thoughts in a safe and comfortable environment, knowing that the convergence of points of view will lead to an approach which takes them all into account. The basis of this thought came from a time years ago when, as part of my training at Neilson/Cadbury, they had us read a book called Mining Group Gold by Thomas Kayser. As I tended to approach most things, with that book, I tried to take away one good usable fact that I could use in the future. That one takeaway was related to the title – in every meeting, every person has a gold nugget that would be on its own, just a small piece of the puzzle. However, when you get a nugget from each person, at the end of the meeting, you would have a pile of nuggets which then became very valuable. I therefore made it my goal in most meetings to do all I could to gather all of those nuggets, and as such, it was very important to me that everyone had a chance to feel safe to express their thoughts. In this particular meeting at Wahl, we conducted the meeting, arrived at our conclusion going forward, and left the meeting. Afterwards, a lady from our finance department came down to my office and raised the possibility that we may have made a wrong choice in our solution. I was happy she was bringing this up because she was trying to protect me from making an error, but I was a bit frustrated as she had been in the meeting and had had every chance to speak up. I asked her why she didn't say something in the meeting. She responded that my personality was such a presence in the room as the Senior guy, and she had sensed that I wanted to go in the direction we went that she didn't want to disagree with me and risk throwing the meeting off the course I wanted it to go. A big learning for me – I had no idea people thought that deeply beyond the issue at hand, that this would come into play. I thought about it, though and realized that yes, I too am very aware of Senior Leaders in meetings and where they want meetings to go. Generally speaking, if it is not a major error in direction, the group will go along because nobody wants to negatively affect their career by taking on the "Big Guy" in a public meeting.

Another aspect of Senior Leadership that is frequently missed is the "Congratulations" for something significant that someone achieves. I can remember many times in my career when an employee of mine did something great. I would write to my Manager, and depending on who I was working for at the time, might include his or her Manager as well, praising my employee and what he or she had achieved. There are several possible wins for the employee who did something great. Step one in this scenario was to show the employee how impressed I was with what they had done. Step two was to show them that it was important enough to include others in my praise. My email and/or public praise would achieve this. Step Three would be if my Manager did something to show that he had received this, read it, and understood it. Step Four could make this an even bigger win – if my Manager felt it significant enough to send it on to his/her Manager. In the case that this happened, Step Five could be an acknowledgment from the Higher-Ups that they, too, had seen it and appreciated the achievement. This could create a situation where one act becomes a major win for an employee. 40 years after I left Kellogg's, my wife still has a file of letters from the Higher-Ups at Kellogg's for acts I did back then. In other words, they meant something to me (I showed my wife), and they meant something to my family – huge win for me. Here is where the impact of leadership comes into play. You can see in the above example that if all works well, it's a very easy major win for the employee, but **also for the company!** What a great message to the employee – do great things and you will be recognized and celebrated (It's probably very good for their career too!)

On the flip side, for the number of times I have seen letters/emails forwarded to the "Higher-Ups," I have seen more often than not crickets from the "Higher-Ups". If this were a Charlie Brown cartoon, you would hear the "womp-womp" sound right now. What a let-down!! So if I can paraphrase the message from the "Higher-ups" that is usually received it goes something like this – "we are too busy to take the time acknowledge this, we have more important things to do than worry about stuff like employees doing great things that oh by the way, will help us succeed even more". The employee could have had a nice, personalized note, even if it just said "Hey, Great job, really impressed with this", which he/she would have for sure shown to his/her spouse, and probably a fellow employee or two and may have even mentioned it to a friend or two. Instead, the "Higher-up" has opened the possibility at least of the employee thinking that everyone up the chain of command acknowledged the achievement, except the people at the top. I don't blame the people at the top, as I said in the respect chapter, many well-intentioned people just don't realize how to show some proactive respect.

Corporate speak

One of the good aspects of writing a book is this Chapter. I am going to call this my self-indulgent chapter. I hate Corporate Speak! I mentioned earlier at Cadbury, when one of my Managers put in a Performance appraisal, "Frank does not suffer fools gladly". In other words, I do not believe in taking oneself too seriously, nor do I tolerate bullshit very easily. Corporate speak runs so counter to everything I want to stand for, I cannot stand it. In my mind, it just shows someone trying to sound important when they really could just say what they want to say in basic English and most likely be a better communicator. My experience was that the larger a group, the more Corporate speak was involved.

In the early days at Wahl, Scott and I would have had to upgrade our speech just to get to "down to earth". The F word was the most frequently used word in our discussions by far, and I am not sure that it ever gave up the #1 spot. We did, however, consider ourselves very down-to-earth, and it worked. We and our teams built one hell of a business by just dealing directly with the issues at hand. Nobody cared if you used college words, or words that sounded good. "Fix the fking problem" was far more effective in our world than "We will do a deep dive to determine root cause". Are you kidding me – root cause??

Some of the phrases that particularly grate on me:

Low-hanging fruit: What are we...cavemen running through the forest??

Circle back: What's wrong with "we will check back in a week". I don't want to run in a circle to get there, I want a direct line!

Bandwidth: The only bandwidth I am familiar with is that which is part of supplying my data capabilities on a phone or computer. I am person with the ability to either squeeze in extra work or not – I don't have fking bandwidth!!

Core competencies: At Kellogg's, I guess they would say their core competency is cereal. I worked there many years before core competency became a thing – we always referred to cereal as our "main business". I guess that didn't sound complicated enough for the latte/Starbucks crowd and their core competencies.

I think you get the idea. That was part of why I had to end up at a company like Wahl Canada, where we were at the beginning, small enough that basic communication and getting things done were all that mattered. As I write this, Scott is President of North America, responsible for the US/Mexico and Canada. In other words, he has been thrust into a vastly different environment from the one we started in. It is impossible for him not to be affected by the environment he is working in. One day, he mentioned to me that we had to meet to see if we were aligned on a particular issue. Needless to say, I razzed him for becoming "one of them". In my world, we talk about agreeing – aligning is for the latte/Starbucks crowd.

Being President

It was near the end of 2016 and I was looking ahead to my last 8 years of my career with a planned retirement date at the end of 2024. I was doing some soul-searching. Scott was President of Wahl Canada but it was a very little part of what he did because so much of that job is what I was doing. He was busy working in Europe, Australia and Asia. I decided to approach him. I told him that I was at the point where I had to decide if I wanted to finish my career as VP of Wahl Canada, or try my hand at running a company. As Scott and I were always open with each other, I told him 'I don't want to leave Wahl Canada but I do think I want to try running a company before I retire so I think I am going to have to leave'. He asked me if I wanted to run Wahl Canada and if that would help me to stay. I said 'Definitely' and in short order, he made that happen.

It is a weird feeling to be President. I had spent my entire career looking up to President and now I was one? I didn't feel like "that Guy". That "Guy" was the guy who always knew how to handle things, who was polished, who was decisive, and who was the guy whose opinions should be listened to because he knows what he is talking about.

Now I was that guy and feeling anything like it. I did not know how to handle things, I was not decisive, and I certainly felt like everyone else's opinions mattered at least as much as mine. I remember hearing from people saying things like "the President's going to be in the meeting" or "the President wants this" and I wanted to scream....."I am just Frank!!!". It was very strange at first. I never really got used to it but I learned to adapt as time went on. I have to confess – I did like hearing the name when I was referred to as President. I worked my whole career so maybe it was kind of nice to hear how far I had come.

Where I really loved being President was the ability to help people without having to ask permission. I mentioned in the book a gentleman who had eye issues and I was able to instantly say "we are going to help you". I loved being able to do that!

I loved it after the Pandemic when we looked around at what our warehouse guys had done for us – I was able to ensure that the 'thank you' was fitting for what they did. They worked through all of the following:

- **Illness**: They and their coworkers were getting COVID and yet they kept coming and shipping product.
- **Demand/staffing**: While we were short-staffed due to illness, and "over-demanded" due to the pandemic, they still performed at the highest levels in the industry. We also, because of safety procedures made their jobs so much tougher and they just fought through it all.

It is hard to describe how you feel about guys like that as President but I was fortunate to be able to find a way for the company to say thanks. We started buying tickets to Blue Jays and Maple Leaf games because our thinking was that the guys in the back usually loved sports, they were not the highest paid part of the company and so therefore, these games might not be affordable to most of them, and that we could give them an experience they might not otherwise have. We started doing that to say thank you and the number of times I heard from our guys that they took at family member down, or a friend and had a great time made it all worthwhile. That is one of the great things about being President.

For most of the time I worked there and even afterwards, it was (and still is) hard for me to say "I was President". It seems to convey things that I don't feel like. I feel like "just a dude" and being "President" seems to convey so much more.

Navigating Friction in a close relationship

In early 2023, Wahl Canada was coming off one of our best years ever for profit and sales. Things were going great. I had not been reporting to Scott for a few years but he was put back in charge of Canada by virtue of being appointed "President of North America" so my position reported into him. I thought "I have a couple of years left in my career so it will be great reporting to Scott to finish out my career". It actually was kind of fitting as it meant I was back to where I started – the Scott and Frank show! As you have no doubt seen throughout my journey, things often change and this one changed in ways neither of us saw coming.

One of the great things about leading a country for the Wahl organization through the years was the ability to do what I thought was right for the business and achieve the results we achieved. In early 2023, that was starting to change in the company. HQ wanted to start to realize the benefits of being a global organization. That meant standards for how we did things so that HQ would know that a Wahl employee in Asia, or Europe or North America would have as close as possible to similar employment experiences with our company. What this meant for me was a changing in the way we did business. I now needed to check a lot more of what I did with HQ, and in some cases, I was not able to do things the way I had in the past – things had to be changed. In a lot of ways this was tough because I was used to being accountable for the company to our employees. In the direction the company was going, I was going to find myself in positions where I had to say "that's what I have to do because the company wants it that way" rather than being wholly accountable. After 6+ years of being the guy making the decisions, it was not easy to have to change. It was made even more complicated because Scott was the guy responsible for ensuring that I was doing things the way the organization wanted. I completely understood why the company was doing what it was doing – if I owned a worldwide company, I would want standards set and upheld so that I was assured of how we were doing business around the world so I don't in any way criticize the direction – it just was not right for me at the time. I was too used to operating the way I did and it had produced some very strong results.

Tensions increased throughout the year as I am certain I was not easy to manage for Scott. I saw this direction the company was going as possibly good for the worldwide organization, but not good for the Canadian employees and the Canadian employees were who I was accountable to in my mind.

Scott and I did come out the other end with our relationship intact and strong and the key to it was that despite being firmly on different ends of the argument, we did try to treat each other with (here comes that word again) respect. We were not always good at it as we had a couple of really good shouting matches and some contentious emails but we did make it out the other end.

One of the important learnings for me throughout was that we always seemed to do better when we were either on video calls, or in person. I think that is because it is easy to hide behind theory and logic in an email when making your point. It is much harder in person because "that's my buddy" so even though you might have a point to make, in person you might soften it a bit because "that's my buddy". If I were to do my career over again, in close relationships, I would try harder to do things face to face rather than emails.

Retirement

A journey that started in September of 1981, ended in July of 2024. It is now March of 2025. For those of you wondering what it is like to be retired, let me offer some limited perspective.

It took me a few weeks to realize, "I never have to get a job again," which, once that sinks in, is a tremendous feeling! I have always heard that perspective changes when you are retired, and it sure does.

Things that used to be a minor part of my day now become major. I used to get up in the morning somewhere between 4-5 and get into the office by no later than 6. When I left the office, I would usually have some of the personal errands to take care of (Shopping,

Doctors, car appts, helping kids, etc). These personal commitments became a minor add-on to what was a fairly busy week. Now, most of these events are a major part of the day. My day now starts around 6-630. I have 2-3 coffees while watching Sportscenter and/or the news. My wife usually comes down around 7:30-8 and we take the dog on a 2.5 km walk. When we get back, we have breakfast and leisurely prepare for our day. After breakfast, I go to my downstairs gym, workout, and then shower after that. By the time this is all done, it is nearly lunchtime! Afternoons are for writing, shopping, and just doing some of the stupid stuff we all do on the computer. In the summers, I golf at least once/week. On top of all this, I have a new Granddaughter

(18 months old), another one due in July, so babysitting is also something new. Man, are Grandkids fun!!

There is a mindset adjustment that goes along with retirement as well. My wife and I were planning an overnight day trip to Eastern Ontario recently (We have a family cottage there she inherited), and she mentioned a date she was thinking of travelling so I could make sure I was able to go. I looked at my calendar and my first reaction was "that's a Monday, we can't go on a Monday.". I actually went back and told her that. She then reminded me that I am retired, and we can go on whatever day we choose – we don't need to choose weekends anymore! I can't believe that 8 months into retirement, my mind didn't process that. Every retirement revelation that comes along hits me in a similar manner – "Wow, that's true!!". I have yet to have a negative revelation. The exception is health – I have for years had a bad back, and it is starting to act up, so that is a concern for my future ability to golf. (a lot of pressure on my chiropractor to allow me to keep having a great retirement!!)

Scott Fraser

I would be remiss without giving Scott his own chapter in this book. I owe him the greatest depth of gratitude for so many things. If not for him, the Wahl part of the journey never would have happened, and I think you can see, the Wahl part of my journey was easily the most important part of my ability to have the life I have enjoyed. It allowed all aspects of my life to be great over the last 25 years:

- **Financially:** I was able to get to the point where I could retire at my goal of 65 years old.
- **Quality of Life:** My career at Wahl started with Scott saying, "I don't care how often you come into the office

as long as you produce the results I think you can". Remember, this was way before "work from home" became a thing during the pandemic. I never abused that privilege, but I was always grateful for the trust that he showed me.

▢**Fun:** Scott showed me that my instincts about laughing and having fun, which previous companies had tried to suppress, were actually effective in making connections and differentiating ourselves from some of the uptight latte/Starbucks crowds we saw way too much of.

▢**Long-term perspective:** I never had a Manager who was able to look beyond the issues of the day and into the longer term as well as Scott did. He was extremely driven to success, wanted it more than anyone I have ever known, but he didn't let that drive affect the way he handled those times when we failed. It is still hard for me to understand how someone could possess the amount of drive that he has, and yet still handle failure as well as he does. I think many Managers could benefit from understanding that if we are trying to walk 10 miles and today we take two steps backwards, that does not mean we will not get to 10 miles, it simply means we will have to take two extra steps to get there.

Most of all, Scott was able to see past the weaknesses that I knew I had and, that the personality test he gave me before I was hired very accurately showed. My guess is 99% of the Managers I worked with would have seen those results, and that would have been it for me. Imagine – you are going to hire someone to handle your money and work with the biggest customers, and you have a test that you trust telling you, "this guy could care very little about risk and he could not find a detail if it came up and bit him in the ankle". I can confidently say that 99% of the Managers I worked with would have said, "No thanks". I will forever be in debt to Scott for making a decision that must have been very concerning at the time.

I hope I didn't let him down. Pull my finger, buddy.

The Journey

The journey started out with a goal. From that first time I saw the Canada Dry salesman and I thought to myself, "here is an easy career for someone with my weaknesses" to 43 years later when I retired as President of Wahl Canada, the goal was always to have a reasonably responsible job and decent enough standard of living when it came time to retire. It was never "I want to be a Company President," but it was always "I want a successful career as a higher-level manager in a company selling mainstream products to consumers". Mission accomplished, but not in the way I had imagined. I had imagined a linear rise to the stop in a similar manner to climbing the ladder. I never foresaw Nivel kicking me off

351

the ladder when they fired me. I never foresaw the sidestep into the partnership at Retail Solutions and having to "retool" my career when it was clear my partner was not up to the challenge. I did not foresee jumping down a couple of rungs (from both a title and financial perspective) on the ladder to a National Account Manager position to start at Swenson Canada (which became Wahl Canada Inc). This was absolutely the right thing to do for a guy who questioned his ability to "get along" in the big corporate world and knew where my strengths were – selling products! It was the wrong thing from the perspective of increasing my earnings at the time or showing progression up the corporate ladder on my resume.

If I could have advised my earlier self at the start of the journey, I would have said the following:

- Early in your career, be more open to feedback. You don't have nearly the answers you think you do! Stop trying to hide your weaknesses – embrace and manage them to minimize the damage they can do. And for God's Sakes, don't be afraid to admit that you have these weaknesses and are doing all you can to manage them.
- You did the right things by choosing big companies early in your career and staying with them for 5 years plus – the number of times afterwards the names Kellogg's and Cadbury made it

easier for people to accept our competency was a big help.

☐I would really have loved to understand respect and helping others succeed as two core principles early on – those two are most critical.

☐Be a bit more cynical about others you come in contact with – as someone with a sunny disposition, you tend to be too trusting of those you deal with. Understand, many of these people do have their own career agendas heavily influencing their actions. It doesn't mean necessarily that you should react differently to them, but sometimes understanding motivations can help you adjust to a situation.

☐Most importantly, do not lose that sense of humour. When

you look back in retirement on your career, while money and success are going to be a part of it, one of the most important questions you will ask yourself is, "Did you have fun?"

I do feel fortunate that I believe I had more fun in my career than most. I was able to, through both luck and hard work, have a career that achieved most of my goals, but also allowed me to have more laughs per hour than just about anyone I know. I remember a young Account Manager we had who respected Scott and I a ton. He got to know us pretty well and knew that we didn't take ourselves too seriously so when an opportunity came to redirect some of that humour at us, he didn't hesitate. Scott and were well known for early morning meetings in his office. We were both early morning people and we enjoyed each other's company so when the second of us arrived, we almost always ended up in each other's office usually discussing the issues of the day but other times just discussing life. For those of you that wonder what kind of high level stuff goes on in meetings between VPs/Presidents this young man has pictorial evidence of what goes on. There is a picture somewhere of the two of us in Scott's office and rather than meeting to discuss something strategic or employee-focussed as often happens, the two of us are bent over looking out his office window. A herd of Canada geese (For all of you shouting at me"Its not a herd, it's a gaggle", I know…

herd just sounds better) had taken over our parking lot so we were spending a lot of high-level mental energy watching the geese. We were shown that picture several times through the years and laughed every time – we looked like such idiots.

I remember flying with Scott one day, and we were on a flight of several hours, and we talked the whole time (mostly business talk), and at the end of the flight, a woman came up to us and asked if we worked together. We said that we did. She said, "That's not fair, nobody should be able to have that much fun and get paid for it". That's how lucky I was!!

In sincere gratitude

To all those who contributed to my ability to have this great career. I have tried to minimize using names in this book so will limit myself to first names only here.

Mike – Early Manager – tough as nails because he could see that was what I needed! You were right about what I needed – thank you. Enjoy life on the boat!

Glenn – Second Manager who opened the door for me not just at Neilson, but to the Big Leagues of selling – I am and will be forever grateful.

Jeff – A partner in crime early in my career – we had so many laughs and became lifelong friends.

John/Mike – One of the key sit-downs of my career – thanks for having the balls to take me down a few pegs

Matt – Fond memories of great times together.

Jack – class act from the start – loved working with you and looked up to you so much.

Greg – you were a one-of-a-kind leader – thank you for supporting me.

Brian – Hard to imagine anyone taking on a job under tougher conditions – thank you for your support.

Karim/Afshan – 2 of my favourite people in 43 years – thank you for everything.

Dorine – Never have I been so wrong about someone in my early evaluation – thank you for simply doing "you" and shoving my words down my throat. You were an absolute pleasure to work with and I loved seeing your success!

Sasan – On my list of "best hires in 43 years," – I appreciate your support and your friendship.

Pam – Also on my list (just behind Sasan of course ☺), stay out of taxis!!! You know how I feel about you ☺.

Paul – I will always remember your tremendous ability to manage so much and always (Okay, almost always) with a smile on your face. Thank you for everything – continued success in your career.

Christina – I never saw anyone give more of themselves to a

company and I will forever appreciate how much you gave up for us. One of my biggest regrets is that we never did say goodbye so I did not get the chance to tell you how I feel. I missed you, I respected you, and I wished, and still wish nothing but happiness for you.

Alvaro – I don't think you ever could imagine the amount of respect I have for you as a person. You are one of the truly great people I have met in 43 years. Thank you for all the blood, sweat and tears you laid down for me.

Bruce (Canada) – In 43 years I never met anyone who didn't know how to say "no" better than you. Thank you for everything!

Maureen – One of the purest souls I met in 43 years. I am so grateful you joined me early on in my journey and were there at the end. You deserve nothing but happiness – thank you for all you did for me.

Nicole – You were an incredibly important part of our team – I wish you nothing but happiness!

Lucy – I was always proud of what we were able to do for you – we could not have done it without your amazing attitude and hard work. Thank you and good luck with the baby and any futures!

Andrea – I could not have made it through the pandemic without you – you saved my sanity and I will always remember that!

Melissa – one of my fellow Obsessive Responsives ☺ I really loved having you as a colleague and friend – Best of luck and happiness to you

Sally – my fellow early "morninger"...you and I "get" each other – we sure had some great laughs! All the best!

Bruce (USA) – Probably the most dynamic personality I met in 43 years – I am grateful for your support of the Canadian team throughout the years.

Ray – You were a great friend and an incredibly interesting personality. I still believe that girl was paid to say that about you 💋 You will never convince me otherwise.

Aldo – There from start to finish – I have so much respect for the way you do business – can't wait to see you join the ranks of the retired.

Bryan – You were one of the absolute "rocks" of the company – so much respect for what you did for us. All the best!

Celine – I am not sure I ever met anyone who lived and died for their customers as much as you did – that explains a lot about your success. I wish you nothing but the best!

Stephen – I think the chapter devoted to you says it all, but if not, I am very glad to have met you and I miss our interactions. God, we had some fun! Bought any good epilators lately?

Lisa – you were there during one of the most fun time periods we had and you were a big part of it. Great memories!

Rich – One of the first people I wanted to hire within 30 seconds and you never disappointed me since then! I very much respected how you faced some of those early challenges.

Singying – One of the true joys from my Asian experience – I wish you nothing but the best!

Ryan – without you, starting out in Asia would have been so much tougher. Thank you for the great understanding you had in knowing the challenges some idiot from Canada would have in figuring out Asia.

Shaun – Came late to my career, but I thoroughly enjoyed our time together

Brett – so glad I got to know you and hope to have more contact in future years!

Martin – I think of you way more than you could imagine and hope the best for you! Miss you and all the laughs we had together.

Colin – You were the best – so much fun and laughter!! A bright light turned off way too soon – RIP, my friend.

Scott A – Wow....did you ever get a lot done in a short period of time – Be Proud my Friend and enjoy retirement!!

Normand – one of the BEST in every way – thank you for all you did for my career – talk soon!

Norma – I think of you often

Sara – I can't think of anyone who is genuinely nicer than you are – I will miss our interactions

Scott F – I covered a lot of my gratitude to you in the book but for whatever I missed – thank you, thank you, and thank you!

To Dianna Emerson – I met Dianna through a Facebook group I joined to try and find out how to be an author. Dianna is the single person most responsible for this book being written. I had no idea if what I was writing would be of interest to anyone, so I wrote a few chapters and went to this group looking for someone to just read it, and let me know if I should continue, or just burn it in the fireplace and have it never surface again. Dianna was so encouraging that it convinced me to stick with it, and she has been a partner in bringing this to completion. I am so grateful, Dianna – your kindness to a complete stranger has been a real boost to a retired guy trying to find his way.

"He Doesn't work"

I am currently 8 months into retirement. The future for me will include cottaging, golfing, spending time with my family and friends – especially the Grandchildren! I loved writing this book, but I think that is probably "all I got" to write about – the rest of my life would probably not hold your interest. I have a great group of buddies, but the audience for those stories would definitely be a limited one. We also have a code that "what goes on with us, stays with us". It can be a serious offence to give up what goes on with this group of about a dozen or so long-time friends.

If I end up doing any kind of work, it will be related to helping others figure out some of the stuff that I was lucky enough to learn in 43 years. I wish I had had someone who was willing to talk about all the things they had been through with an eye towards helping me get that learning as early as possible. There is no reason I should have had to wait until the last part of my career to learn about a concept as powerful as respect. If I can help others learn things that more quickly, I am all in! This could take the form of public speaking, coaching or any other kind of format that comes along. If you have any opportunities you want me to consider, please reach out to the contact details below. I will leave you with this – in her Grade 9 year, we had a "take your daughter to work day". I was thrilled. She came in and had a very informative day. When we got home at the end of the day and my wife asked how things went at Dad's work, her answer was "He doesn't work, all he does is stand around and tell jokes all day". I am so lucky to have been able to have that kind of fun at work for most of my career.

I am extremely grateful that you took the time to read this gibberish –if you want to address me directly, feel free to. I do respond to all messages because, well, it's the respectful thing to do ☺ If you want to review this book, good or bad, it is appreciated. It has been my honour to experience this journey and I hope you enjoyed the parts I could bring you along on. I sincerely thank you for taking your time to read this.

Email: frb59personal@gmail.com

LinkedInprofile:
https://www.linkedin.com/in/frank-brown-37145911b/